HIDDEN M

SURVIVING, HEALING AND RISING FROM THE ASHES OF ABUSE

By
John Two-Hawks

CSR Media

A Division of Circle Studios Records

Wopila (great thanks) to:

Marsia Geldert-Murphey – Proofing / Editing
Nora Viola Photography – Front Cover photo
John Rankine, Nora Viola – Back Cover photos
Josh Kolb – 'Hidden Medicine' Cover Text
CSR Media – Graphic Design / Layout
Joseph Chamberlain – Original Art

I never thought I would write this book. Then, a number of years ago I read *The Little Prisoner*. The author had to use a pseudonym – Jane Elliott – to protect herself from her abuser. I want to thank Jane for her courage, as reading her book helped me to find mine. It planted a seed in me, and that seed has now bloomed into the flower that is *Hidden Medicine*.

- John Two-Hawks

Thank you to Enya.
Your music infused my words with feeling.

Dedicated to my brother and sisters
Together we rose from the ashes

For Peggy
Your love has always been my hidden medicine

You have to look deeper, way below the anger, the hurt, the hate, the jealousy, the self-pity, way down deep where the dreams lie. Find your dream. It is the pursuit of your dream that heals you.

~ Billy Mills – Oglala Lakota

Hidden Medicine
~ Prologue ~

And so the secrets can no longer hide in the shadows. The time has finally come for me to shine light into the darkness, to write down and share what happened to me all those years ago. I want to tell you that I am not writing this book to settle a score or exact some sort of retribution. I am a healed and victorious man, and I have long since left those unhealthy reflexes behind. I am writing this for two reasons: the first is the simple fact that I have been silent about it for too long. The second is that I hope; by sharing my story, anyone who has a secret story of their own may find their hidden medicine within. This true account will not be told chronologically, but topically. So the timeline will be less a line and more a circular wave, as if we are sitting in a room having a fireside chat, reflecting on the experiences of darkness and light that shape us and make us who we are. So here we go....

My father died at age 54. The next year my mother died at age 51. Soon after my mother's death I found myself entering a sacred, ceremonial ground with three medicine people. We were there to pray; to seek guidance from Spirit. At this point in my life I had come to almost expect that, for whatever reason, things just never really went my way. Bad luck seemed to follow me around wherever I went, and I had developed a kind of helpless resignation about my tendency toward misfortune. The death of both my young parents within one year sure seemed like just another example of that hard reality. On that day in that sacred area, there were some remarkably beautiful spaces, and I felt drawn to go to one of those places to pray, but it was not to be. Instead, I found myself being taken to the most broken down, craggy, uncomfortable and unbeautiful area in the whole place! As I began to softly bemoan the reasons why, a bright red cardinal landed on a rock just a few feet from where I stood and began to sing to me very excitedly. It was at that moment that over twenty years of pain and loss rose to the surface and poured out of me. Spirit reached into my aching soul and touched me with a profound truth that opened my heart for transformation and imbued my spirit with a deep wisdom that has never since left me. It is that gift that I wish to share with you in this book. It is that gift I wish to impart with the music that tells this story.

As I stand on this high plain of experience with the sturdy legs of perseverance and look over the span of my life, I can see so much. I understand so much. I can see the little 4-year-old boy who heard the music and knew it was his destiny. I now understand the meaning of his first vision at six years of age, when tatanka (buffalo) visited him in a powerful dream. I now know that the spirit of tatanka was sent to protect him. I can see the fear and confusion that began to take root in the boy when his parents divorced right after that vision, and his life was turned upside down as his young mother moved him and his younger siblings from place to place, never able to pay the rent or choose a decent man, or stay away from bad medicine. I can see how the boy loved her, and how he needed her, and how it broke his heart when she gave him away. I now understand her reasons why, and I really never blamed her despite having good reason to. But in the end my mother failed her children terribly. So many of her choices were selfish and destructive, and ultimately led to the madness that would eventually do so much damage to me and my siblings. I can see that sensitive 8-year-old boy moving for the 13th time into a house with his dad and new step-mother Emily, and facing yet another school full of scary kids and the meanness of life. I see, and want so bad to protect him from more pain, but alas I cannot. I can understand the meaning of his second vision at age nine, in which a sad old man visited him right after he and his siblings moved into that house with his father and Emily. I now know that the spirit of that elder was sent to warn him about what was coming. I can see how it all started then, the subtle descent from the appearance of normalcy into a living hell, as the veneer of false niceties wore off the new wife and were replaced with a seething, maniacal hate and perverse madness. And I can see how he loved his dad and felt sorry for him as he struggled with substance abuse and the quiet desperation of a job he often said he hated. I can understand his reasons why now – and again – I never really blamed him although I certainly had reason to. My father's escape was alcohol and drugs. He was a kind, gentle and passive man and I loved him dearly, but he never made the madness being inflicted on his children stop even though he knew it was happening. Instead, he chose to look the other way, and thus failed his children in that regard. I hold no ill will toward my dad. He worked hard to keep a roof over our head and feed us, and I honor that. But other than a few shining moments of courage which I will tell you about later, he made choices that directly contributed to the suffering his children endured. I can see it all so clearly from this vantage point. I see where the bad luck I became so accustomed to in my life began. I see where it all started. The hidden medicine I found within that day in that craggy sacred place was borne of this torturous journey. I know, it is more than ironic and maybe even a bit hard to fathom, but it is the truth. The seed for great power and courage which would be realized decades later was sown during this period of deep suffering and fear. Thus, I look back to tell you how it all happened. To lay it all bare in the hopes that you may find your own courage, and your own healing. Yes, I see it all so clearly now. But back then the seed, that would one day become my hidden medicine, was still concealed in the shadows....

Of Shadow and Light

~ Finding the God Fingers in the Darkness ~

As I recall it, my childhood was quite normal and happy for the first five or six years. The firstborn of four children, I was conceived in the heat of passion by a 16-year-old girl and a 20-year-old young man. A rushed marriage and three more children followed over the next 5 years. I have often joked that I was present at my mom and dads wedding (in the womb), and even had some cake! I have fond sun-bleached memories of those early years that appear in my minds-eye like the fading color of an old photograph. The sounds of carefree laughter echo in my ear like a long-forgotten dream. I remember playing football in the yard at our house out in the country on a sunny afternoon with my little brother, giggling uncontrollably as 5 and 3 year old boys do when our dad, on his knees, tackled us as we tried to run by. I remember learning to ride my bike and falling down in the grass over and over and over. I remember my mom, who we all called 'Mumma' even into adulthood, teaching me at the kitchen table how to color outside the lines and draw an abstract. I also remember her long dark hair, the un-tucked flannel shirts and bell-bottomed jeans she would wear when she took me for walks in the woods to hunt for Morel mushrooms. She was so earthy, and always seemed to know where the mushrooms were. Those walks were the first times I would hear about our American Indian lineage. My mom didn't say a lot, but she said enough to instill in me an early sense of some idea of Native identity that would one day become the beacon which would light the way home. There were sad moments too. My first pet was a beagle puppy I named 'Rascal'. One day I came home from kindergarten to have my mother sadly tell me that he had been hit by a school bus and killed. But even the shadows of that moment were enveloped with the God fingers of light and love, as my mom helped me through my first experience with death. And I will never forget the magic of Christmas during those years. There were colorful, twinkling lights, shiny gold and silver garland, and Mumma would make these amazing ornaments from eggshells complete with little scenes inside. She made a Santa in a wooden rocking chair all by hand, and a candy-cane style wall hanging out of yarn. My mom was an artist through and through. I have both of those items today, and I put them out every year and they remind me of those happy times. My dad always went all out, buying us lots of gifts, and we were always so excited on Christmas morning to see and open our presents. Of all the warm reflections of those first 6 years, the most meaningful to me are those times when my dad would set up his amplifier, guitar and microphone in the living room, and he and Mumma would sing songs and encourage me to sing too. There is an old recording that will one day find its way onto one of my albums. It is of me, at 5 years of age, singing *You Are My Sunshine* while my dad plays his guitar. So, you see, it has always been music right from the start.

In those formative years, I also spent a lot of time in the woods exploring, and it was there, in the quiet of nature, that I made my earliest connection with Tunkasila (Grandfather/Creator) and with my own spirit. I was born a very sensitive soul. I was never the boy who engaged in roughhousing or aggressive behavior. My mother once told me that I came into the kitchen one day with blood running down my face. As she rushed to my side and asked me what happened, I replied that my little brother had hit me over the head with a toy tractor! I did not cry, and I did not retaliate. Not because I was a saint, but because I was *afraid*. From the beginning and as you will see throughout my life, fear has always been present. Finding the courage to face it has been a lifelong journey. Quiet reflection, not loud aggression, was my true nature, and back then there was just no place for a sensitive boy. Sensitive boys got bullied, beat up and picked on, and I endured decades of that treatment. I have also never been a social butterfly, and have always preferred being by myself. In my efforts to fit in I would sometimes try to play the part of what I saw as the 'typical' male, but it was all just an act. Truthfully, I just longed for my quiet space alone where I could be myself. I once sat on the step of our front door at that country farmhouse and watched birds in a tree for over two hours. That's the kind of boy I was. The natural world was fascinating, safe and kind and that's where I wanted to be. No one would be mean to me there. Birds would sing their songs to me. The leaves would rustle and soothe. The breezes would kiss my face and play with my golden hair. That was my world. That was where I felt the most at home. However, that was all about to change....

I don't recall the moment my parents got divorced. I also have no recollection of the day we moved out and went with our mom, or where exactly we ended up. This is the period of my life when small details get lost in the blur of confusion. All I can tell you is that we moved, a lot. We moved so often I sometimes lost track of where I was. I got into a habit of planting a seed from an apple in the yard at each place we moved into. I would water it and check on it daily. I don't recall anything ever growing, but it prompted my mom to dub me 'Johnny Appleseed'. I guess I was subconsciously trying to put down roots. I also began collecting mementos and saving them in what I called my 'memory bag'. I still have that bag to this day. One afternoon when I was in 2nd grade, I froze in the hallway because I got confused about which school I was in. It was a frightening moment for an 8-year-old. We would move in to a new place, be there for a short while, and then the landlord would kick us out, or Mumma would move us to get away from a bad boyfriend. And there were plenty of bad boyfriends. My mom was pretty, young and needy and she attracted losers like flies on sticky strips. One of those losers was Randy. He had long blonde hair and would hang around all hours of the day. I didn't like him. He made me uncomfortable for some reason. Then one afternoon, I went down into the basement for something I can't remember anymore. But what I will never forget as long as I live is what my young eyes witnessed when I got to the bottom of those stairs. It is like a flash in my mind now, but that flash is seared into my memory. The blonde boyfriend, his pants down, my little sister, her wide, terrified eyes.... It was the end. The end of innocence. The end of happy. The end of childhood. Nothing would ever be normal again.

I put my finger under Mummas nose to see if she was still breathing. She had been sleeping on the sofa for two days and nights and hadn't stirred though I had shaken her and loudly called her name. I was really scared that she might be dead. I felt her breathe, and breathed my own sigh of relief. But my siblings and I were hungry, and there was nothing in the house but a few condiment bottles in the fridge and a jar of peanut butter in the cupboard. So, in the middle of summer, I put on a winter coat and walked to the small grocery store a block away. I went in with one thing in mind – steal a loaf of bread. I figured we could at least have peanut butter toast! I went to the aisle where the bread was, looked around, and quickly grabbed a loaf of Wonder Bread and crammed it into my coat. I was so nervous I was shaking. I made my way for the door, trying not to look suspicious (in my winter coat in July). I'm not sure how, but I made it out of the grocery store with that loaf of bread, albeit a bit flattened, but all that really mattered was that it was edible! We had weirdly shaped peanut butter toast that day, and later on my mom finally woke up! There were moments like these throughout those crazy years. Moments when a ray of light cut through the shadows and something good happened, when there was laughter and we were happy for a while. It was during one of those happy times that Mumma put a 45 of Paul Simon's '50 Ways to Leave Your Lover' on the record player and proceeded to teach me how to dance. I'll never forget her putting her hands on my hips and telling me "wiggle your butt"! If you've ever seen me move and sway to the music in concert, you can credit my mom for that! I learned afterward that the reason she had blacked out for nearly 3 days was likely because of some drug she was on. I'll never know for sure. I was only 7.

There were other boyfriends, lots of them. Then along came a guy that looked a lot like Rod Stewart. His name was Wayne and he was a charming, handsome devil and my mother fell for him. In fact, he became my mother's second husband. We moved again into a small cabin in the woods and I was enrolled in yet another new school. At first, the new husband seemed cool to a little boy. He had a shiny car and would take me for rides in it and squeal the tires for me. He also taught me how to make a paper airplane, and helped me put together my very first model car. He seemed nice and friendly at the start. But that didn't last. My second pet was a black and white kitten I named 'Fuzzy'. One day Wayne told me that my kitten had a fractured foot and picked up Fuzzy and told me to come with him. He led me out back behind the cabin, placed Fuzzy on the ground and picked up a ball bat. What ensued I will not describe. I will only say that as I write this now, I am finding it hard to see the screen for the water in my eyes. It still breaks me completely. It was the most horrific experience of my life. Then one night I was awakened by a thumping sound. I got up and went to the doorway of my bedroom and quietly witnessed my mom being punched and slapped by this man. My mother's beautiful face was bloody and battered. I wanted to do something so badly, but I was only 8.

The next day I snuck a steak knife from the kitchen and tucked it inside my coat. I carried it with me secretly everywhere for a while, even to school. I had made a promise to myself that if I ever saw that man hit my mom again I would make sure he stopped. Not long after that we went for one of our regular weekend visits with my dad. At some point he found out about the knife and took it from me. When he asked me why I had it, I could only say "for protection". I was afraid to tell him the real reason. It was about this time that my dad had remarried a woman 10 years younger than him, which meant she was only 10 years older than me. Her name was Emily, and she seemed nice at first. Of course, I had already seen how quickly that could change, but I tried my best to like her. One night, after only a couple weekend visits with my dad and his new wife, Mumma sat down with all four of us kids and asked us, if we could choose to live with her or our dad, who would we choose? She assured us that she would not be upset no matter what we said. For reasons that children shouldn't have to think about, we told her that night we would choose to go live with our dad. Once she left the room I immediately sensed something was wrong, so I went to see and found my mom in the kitchen crying. It broke my heart that I had hurt her like that. I told her that I really wanted to live with her, but it was too late, the damage had been done. My mom took me in her arms and held me, assuring me she was okay, and that she was just sad, that was all. It was during our next weekend visit with my dad that Mumma called and told my dad that if he didn't take full custody of us four kids immediately, we would end up in foster care. Years later I heard that my dad had promised his new 18-year-old wife that she would never have to worry about raising 4 kids because his ex-wife had custody. Well my mother's phone call had sure upended that arrangement. My sister told me she overheard my dad and Emily arguing that night, and that he had said "I don't want them either, but they are my kids and foster care will split them up." So there you have it – nobody really wanted us. I'll never know what he finally said to Emily to appease her, but I do give him at least some credit for not totally abandoning us in that moment. So, what began as a weekend visit turned into more than a decade. And we didn't know it then, but an ominous shadow was about to completely overtake our lives.

'God fingers' is a figure of speech used to describe what are known in the scientific community as crepuscular rays. The rays are atmospheric optics, which appear when light from the sun breaks through dense cloud cover and causes multiple shafts or beams of light. Sometimes in this life, we find ourselves in places of darkness. And that darkness can overwhelm us. But often, just when we need it most, the 'God fingers' appear, and remind us that even the greatest shadows can be penetrated by the light. As in, right in the midst of our greatest fear, sorrow or pain, a blessing will come like a ray of light to give us hope. The blessing may seem like a small thing, but it means everything to anyone who finds themselves beneath the cloud of despair. Throughout all the experiences of my early life, so many of which were terribly traumatic, there have always been moments of hope, reprieve and blessing. These are the God fingers, and they appear when we need them most, helping us to find the strength to carry on when the darkness becomes a burden our soul can no longer bear without the light....

Young Old Soul
~ Innocence Lost, Wisdom Found ~

Something happens in the heart of a child who sees too much too soon. Aside from the obvious mental distress, there is a deeper, more profound effect that is harder to see. A seed is planted in the soul by those things, and if fortunate enough to be watered with love before it dries up and withers away, that seed has the potential to one day sprout into the beginnings of wisdom. As I said before, it is more than a little ironic, but it's true. However, if that seed is not watered, it can – and often does – grow into something destructive. By the time I had moved in to my dad's new house in a quiet, small town village in Michigan, I had seen more in my 8 years than a boy that age should. Fear and distrust had taken hold of my psyche, and the idea of yet another new school with strange kids and teachers whose names I would have to learn filled me with nervous apprehension. I had lost any fondness I might have had for school years earlier. Let me go back and tell you how that all happened….

It was my first day of kindergarten, and I was excited. Mumma had packed my sack lunch and I was standing at the end of our dusty country driveway watching the sun rise, listening to the birds sing, and waiting for the bus. She took a photo of me that morning to commemorate my big moment. That image is on the back cover of this book. I remember being happy as I saw the bus appear down the road, heading my way. As it grew larger and larger, I grew more and more happy. Then it crested the hill, came into full view, and promptly drove right on by me! I was sad and confused. I ran back to the house and told my mom, after which she called the school to tell them what had happened. She was not happy about it, and because I was a bit upset, she let me stay home that day. By the next morning, Mumma had me all jazzed up again, and assured me that the bus would stop for me on this day. So there I was on day two, lunch sack in hand, filled with anticipation. The bus appeared as it had the day before, lumbered toward me, and then drove right by me again! This time I was crushed. Mumma came running out of the house and took me in her arms and I cried the way a boy can only cry when his mother holds him. My mom was furious, and after a loud, angry phone call an arrangement was made. And so it was that the Principal came all the way out to our house in the country and drove me to my first day of school. Mumma followed in her car, and then stood in the back doorway of the classroom once I was in my seat to be sure that I was okay. As the morning proceeded, I kept looking back to see if she was still there. Then came the moment when I turned to look and she was gone. After a few more worried glances it sank in that I was alone. No more Mumma. No more dad. No more little brother and sisters. No more birds to sing to me, or trees to dance for me. I was surrounded by kids in cold, square rows of hard chairs, but I never felt lonelier. As this realization caused feelings of deep sadness to begin to well up inside me, I felt myself about to cry. At that instant, I happened to turn and look at the girl sitting beside me, and her disgusted expression stopped my tears in their tracks. Then during recess on that day, I was bullied and ridiculed by a very big kid and his pals. And so it was, that my happy hopes for school perished, and a new cold reality took hold in me; I would have to hide to survive....

So as I prepared to enter 3rd grade in this new school, I had no naïve excitement about it. I can remember my dad driving me and showing me the 10 block route I would have to walk to get to the elementary school each morning. He made sure to remind me that, as the oldest sibling, I would be responsible for making sure my brother and sisters got to school without getting lost. Then there was the new house. It was nice enough; two stories, a front and back porch, a detached garage and a concrete driveway. It was in town and had two large yards on each side. Compared to the meager, dilapidated cabin and all the other broken-down places we had lived with our mom, this house, which in reality was rather humble, seemed quite fancy to me. We had lived in poverty with Mumma. It seemed things would be much better here. There were 3 bedrooms upstairs. My brother and I got one, my sisters got another, and the largest bedroom was reserved for my dad and his wife Emily, who would now be our step-mother. My sisters got separate bunk-beds for their room, but my brother and I were to share a full size bed. That was a bit odd I suppose, but considering the craziness of my life up to that point, it was not all that strange by comparison. We didn't know it then, but my brother and I would sleep in that same bed for the next decade.

The first weeks and months in our new living arrangement did not leave any lasting impressions, so it is safe to say that things started out as normally as could be expected. School was no fun, but that was nothing new for me. However, sometime after that initial period, things began to change in the home. The niceties and normalcy Emily displayed at the start began to wear off, and were slowly supplanted by perverse, weird and scary behavior. I was 9, and my little brother and I were in the bathtub. Emily had run the bath, told us where the soap and towels were, and left us to take it from there. Then, a short bit after we had gotten into the tub, she unexpectedly popped into the bathroom. Her sudden entrance startled me and I quickly covered my private parts with a washcloth. I was old enough that I did not want to be seen naked, much less by this woman who was still very much a stranger to me at that point. Not to mention that a previous girlfriend of my dad's had forcibly removed my underwear during a violent episode just a couple years earlier. And so I hid myself. She responded by reaching down and yanking the washcloth away from me. As I attempted to hide my genitals with my hands, she told me that I didn't need to do that because "it wasn't anything she hadn't seen before". The washcloth was not returned to me, and as she weirdly lingered in the bathroom, leaving only for moments at a time, I tried my best to keep myself covered as I nervously washed up, got out and dried off. I felt exposed, humiliated and violated. This would be the first among many years of strange and sexually perverse things Emily would subject me to. Around that same time began the setting of bizarre house rules. First there was the rationing. There would only be <u>one</u> roll of toilet paper allowed for four kids per month. Run out before the month was up and you did not get a replacement. This toilet paper rationing was actually marked on a calendar as 'TP'. Add to that the disgusting rule that we were only allowed to flush the toilet once a day, and you can begin to imagine how awful it got. Emily would dole out all food. We were not allowed under any condition to open the cupboard or refrigerator and get food for ourselves. To do so was to risk severe punishment. No electric plugs were allowed for anything, lights were required to be turned off whenever we left a room or suffer the consequences. Sometimes she would turn a light on and claim one of us did it so she could terrorize us. There were also the assigned stools in the kitchen (chronological), and we were regularly expected to pick up fuzz and lint off our bedroom floors on our hands and knees to save her having to "waste electricity" with the vacuum cleaner. These are just a few of the warped house rules she began to impose on us shortly after we moved in and my dad went off to work. We were not allowed to bathe but once a week (on Sunday) and had to take showers together – me with my brother – in order to "save water". My sisters took their showers together too. When we were still small enough, me and my brother would take our weekly shower together, *with* my dad. We could barely all fit in that shower, and it was incredibly awkward to be that close to your fully naked father. The fact that my dad would agree to such a thing speaks to the control Emily had, and to my father's weakness and the role he played in our continuing mistreatment and abuse. He just wouldn't or couldn't make it stop. In some ways, Emily abused him too. These things were just the very beginning of the madness that was to come. They were the setup – the bait and switch. They were the groundwork being laid for the framework that would form the invisible bars from which we would almost never break free. My siblings and I were damaged goods. At ages 4, 5, 6 and 8, we had arrived with already broken souls into my dad and Emily's world from three years of confusion and neglect with our mother. Already having suffered abuse, we were easy prey for a predator. We were pliable material for a madwoman to manipulate. And she did so methodically, bit by bit, adding a rule here and a limit there as time went on, each progressively more warped than the next. And with every new, increasingly sadistic condition, the house, which at first seemed so nice, began to lose its luster and the graying gloom of its walls slowly closed in until we found ourselves physically and mentally imprisoned by the evil web of hate this child abuser had weaved into and around us. We were trapped. There was no escape.

Early on, I found out that my Grandpa lived a short bike ride from our house, and that my Grandma lived only a few blocks away (they had divorced decades earlier). Both were my mother's parents, so I often went to visit them in secret so as to not risk stirring anything up with my dad. There were so many secrets in those years, and so much hiding. My dad was not a mean-spirited man, but he was not overly fond of many of my maternal relatives, which included my Grandmother. He also bore some resentment toward my mother which was faintly visible whenever they saw each other during pickups for weekend visits. Needless to say, I usually refrained from telling anyone when I decided to sneak away to see either of my maternal Grandparents. It was during one of those early visits with my Grandfather that I first heard the stories of our Lakota family lineage, which my mother had alluded to during those Morel mushroom hunts years earlier. Grandpa didn't always speak of it, and he never spoke of it when others were around. It was like a deep chest of mysteries that could only be opened when it was safe, and I innately understood, as the need for hiding was something life had already taught me. I didn't know it then, but there were painful reasons for that secrecy that were born of a legacy of racial discrimination. Let me just say right here that being a Native person of 'mixed blood' is no easy road. The issue of identity is complicated, and can take a lifetime to sort out. Those early realizations of my own Native identity were gradual, and took time to take root in me. But there was something in the learning that I clung to from the start, and it was that there was a tangible explanation for why I was different; why the birds, trees and winds had always been my true friends, and why I had never 'fit' into the square hole the world seemed hell-bent on forcing me into – I was round! The knowledge of that indigenous ancestral link would become an anchor that I would hold onto, and a quiet strength I would draw from during the madness of the years to come, and it would one day call me home and set me free. During one of my first visits with my Grandpa I told him about some of the horrors I had witnessed in the years with my mom, and shared a bit about what was just beginning to become a nightmare living with Emily. When I finished telling him, he got down on one knee and looked at me with a sadness in his face I have never forgotten. As he shook his head and tussled my hair with his thick, dark leathery working hand, he simply said "ohh Johnny, you're a little old man." I didn't know what he meant then. I did not yet know that my innocence had been stolen and my boyhood cut short. Nor did I understand that my young soul had been made old by the terrible things I had seen. But then the journey into the long night, and back to the light, had only just begun.

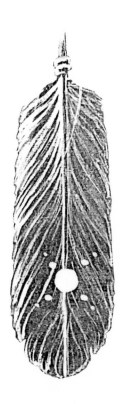

The Long Walk
~ The Birth of Perseverance ~

On the list of incredible life moments I have to cherish are: having my music featured on an Emmy® nominated film score, receiving Grammy® and Native American Music Awards nominations, getting a platinum album award, performing with my friends from the band *Nightwish* for 11,000 fans in Helsinki, Finland, and more. To the casual observer, it might seem as though I live a charmed life. And certainly I have a lot to be thankful for these days. However, there is always more to the story than meets the eye. So I want to take you behind the curtain of performance, past the veneer of persona and give you an all-access pass to the back stage, where everything that made the show even possible still lives.

I am the long-shot, the walk-on, the underdog. I was never the first pick, nor the favorite, and I was never the one expected to win. Nothing, and I do mean *nothing*, has come easy for me. Ever feel like that? As I alluded to earlier, it was like the cards were always stacked against me no matter what I did. I had to claw my way, tooth and nail, to every milestone, every accomplishment, however small, working twice as hard as the next guy for half the gains. I never had a handout, nor had anyone to show me the way. I once had someone give me the proverbial pat on the back as they told me how proud I should be that I 'pulled myself up by my bootstraps.' Though well intentioned, that statement always bothered me and it took me years to sort out why. I now know the reason it didn't sit right with me is that I didn't have any 'bootstraps' to pull myself up with. That comment assumed to know something about my life, and de-legitimized everything it took for me to rise up from the ashes. I am not seeking pity, nor am I in any way looking for praise, but I will admit that sometimes, when I think of the treacherously steep uphill journey I took to arrive where I am today, I do feel a sense of pride. I made it. Against all odds – and with a lot of help – I made it. Damn right. And I'm not done yet. But back then the climb had only just begun.

I didn't know it, but I had it in me from the start; the fuel for a fire that, if lit, would burn long and strong for a lifetime. I think we all have that to some extent, but it doesn't always find the right environment in which to ignite. That quality, that flame I speak of, is *perseverance* – dogged, unrelenting, quiet, steady, defiant determination. The kindling was put in place during those crazy years with my mother and the ensuing decade of abuse that followed....

So the days of my boyhood in Emily's twisted world turned into weeks, then months, and then years; during which time the regimented diet of abuse and madness took its toll, and became the norm. It is a terrible thing for a child to be mentally and emotionally lobotomized, little by little, to have hopes of love and family slowly drowned in the poisoned waters of sadistic evil, and for that evil to become the accepted reality. Years later, breaking the chains of that normalized depravity would prove to be a monumental battle. There was a square metal heat register in the floor of the bedroom I shared with my brother that looked down into a room my dad had made into a 'den' of sorts. It was where he kept all his sports trophies, his collection of records and record player, a 1966 Supro amplifier and he and his father's instruments which included guitars, a banjo and a violin. It was from this 'den' that Emily would scream up through the register into our room "you kids get up!!" every school morning, always jarring me from a deep sleep to begin my day with a mean, loud voice dripping with disdain and dislike for me and my siblings. My sisters' room was situated so that they had to go through the bedroom my brother and I shared to get to the bathroom and to the stairs, which later on would present real privacy issues for us all, some of which Emily would deviously exploit. Heading down the stairs for breakfast on school mornings was horrible. The stairs reached the main floor at the front door, and then there was the living room, then the dining room, and finally the kitchen where our bowls of cereal would be waiting for us at our assigned stools. There was a rickety metal rocking chair just behind the wall in the corner of the dining room that Emily would be sitting in nearly every morning. She was almost always angry, which made every step down those stairs an act of courage. As we would approach the dining room, you could see her pasty white feet sticking out past the wall as she rocked in that old chair and it made that unnerving creaky sound. We would quietly file by her, and I never made eye contact because it was scary to look at someone who hated you so much. Living with this woman was like living with a schizophrenic demon. Some days, for reasons unexplained, she would wake up in a chipper mood and be extra nice to us, which made me even more nervous because I didn't want to mess up and cut our grace period short. Then, the next day, it would be back to the 'usual' treatment. I don't remember when it started, but not long after the abusive norm set in, my brother and I both began having issues with enuresis (bedwetting). I was about 10 or 11 years old, and had not had this problem before I moved in with my dad and Emily. Medical literature about bedwetting lists the following as possible causes: *"Emotional trauma, a stressful home life, major changes, such as starting a new school or moving to a new home, and children who are being physically or sexually abused sometimes begin bedwetting."* Well, all of the above applied at that time in my life, so it is for certain that emotional trauma is what brought it on for me. The days when I wet the bed were awful. The bedwetting itself was bad enough, as waking up in that state makes for a miserable start to your day. But that was only where the misery began. Emily would always be angry about it, yelling and calling me names. It was humiliating to be told that you were so lazy that you would rather urinate on yourself than go to the trouble of getting up out of bed to use the bathroom. It made me feel like there was something really wrong with me. To add insult to injury, Emily would not wash the sheets for weeks. She made me put a plastic bucket underneath the urine soaked bed sheet to hold it up so that by the evening it would be dry, and I would go to sleep that night on those same unwashed sheets. That was the routine. And you've already heard that we were only allowed to bathe once a week, so you get the picture. Those circumstances made school days almost unbearable, as the abuse that started at home just continued at school. Kids can be brutal. The enuresis finally stopped in my mid-teens after I came down with a terribly painful urinary tract infection (which would last 8 years, for reasons I will divulge later). I would begin to urinate in my sleep and the intense burning sensation would awaken me, thus preventing me from completely wetting the bed. I often wonder how long the enuresis would have continued had it not been for that urinary tract infection. I have always had oily skin, so the combination of my naturally oily skin, bedwetting, and once-a-week bathing made for a very unclean and unkempt young boy. Puberty arrived when I was 12, and I developed terrible acne. By

Tuesdays or Wednesdays on a weekly basis my hair would be so greasy it was impossible not to notice. I did try to remedy the situation throughout my teens. There was no way for me to take a towel from home without Emily finding out, so I don't recall anymore where I got it, but somehow I managed to acquire a towel that I kept with me. I would arrive at school and hurry to the boys' restroom, wait till the coast was clear and then quickly dip my head in the sink. I would use that towel to dry my hair. It wasn't much, and it didn't work that well, but it was better than nothing. After that I would rush to hang the towel in my locker and try to make it to my first period class on time. Needless to say, I was tardy a lot, and teachers would scold me about it. They never knew why I was late to class, and I never told them. It was far too embarrassing. One time at high school a creative writing teacher named Ms. Pohl verbally humiliated me in front of the whole class, telling me not to lean my "greasy head" against the back wall. A murmur of giggles could be heard, and I could have cried I was so hurt. Thus, by the time I reached high school my self-esteem was so badly damaged I could barely function normally. I had a terribly negative body-image, and hated my reflection. I was scared of everything and everyone, and became severely introverted. The years of maniacal abuse had done its job. But I'm getting ahead of myself. There is more I need to tell. Much, much more....

His name was Stikine, which my dad said was a Tlingit word. He was a huge animal, half wolf and half Alaskan malamute. He was large framed and tall like a wolf, and thickly muscled like a malamute. But he was a gentle giant who never once gave me reason to fear him. In fact, I loved him. One summer day we kids were outside when we caught the scent of something cooking. As I said, there were weird moments when Emily would do nice things, like actually cook us a meal. So when she yelled for us to come in and eat, I thought it was one of those days and that we might be getting a hot lunch. Now you must understand, that during summer vacations, nearly every day we were served the same thing for lunch: a bologna sandwich on white bread, some potato chips and a small glass of Kool-Aid, and that was it. No seconds or alternative options. As a result, I spent most of my youth hungry and severely underweight. So when we were called in for lunch on this day, the thought of a hot meal had me positively salivating. I made my way to the back door along with my brother and sisters and entered the kitchen expecting to find a freshly cooked dish of some kind awaiting us. But to my utterly confused disappointment, there sat the same old bologna, chips and Kool-Aid lunch we usually got. I was baffled. We all were. There was obviously something cooking in the oven, but there at our assigned stools was the usual meal. Not a word was said about it. We all just quietly took our seats and began eating. Shortly after we sat down, Emily came into the kitchen. She grabbed a pot holder, opened the oven door and reached in to pull out a pizza. I started to get excited at the thought of getting to eat a slice of it, but my excitement was short lived. Emily turned and placed the freshly cooked pizza on the kitchen floor, went out the back door and momentarily returned with Stikine, at which point it sank in; *the pizza was for the dog*, not us. I will never forget the wide eyed, aghast look of silent horror on my sister's face as the dog started eating. It was so bizarre to sit there and chew on a bologna sandwich while hearing Stikine lapping at the pizza on the floor. It was surreal, and it made me feel despised and worthless. These were the kinds of wildly depraved things Emily did to us throughout the years.

I have always loved making model cars. In fact, I still have all but one of the models I made throughout my boyhood and into my teen years. Let me tell you about the one I don't have. I worked so diligently on that model car. It was not from a box, it was a car that I created from the spare parts I collected from other models I had built. So it was an original, and I was extremely proud of it. It was black and silver, with shiny mag wheels and a sweet engine. I dreamed up a cool paint job, and hand painted it to perfection. It was the crown jewel of all my models. As with most instances where Emily inflicted her perverse, abusive punishment, I have no recollection as to what I did to enrage her that day. Whatever it was, she employed her usual routine of slapping my face, then forcing me to pull my pants and underwear down so she could spank my bare bottom with her hand, after which she stormed out of my room. A few minutes later, she burst through my bedroom door, red faced and still infuriated. When I saw it I wailed as I desperately pleaded with her through my tears not to do it. She had my prized model car in her hands, raised it up in front of me, and despite my cries, with a wicked grin on her sinister pale face, she broke it in half. When that model car snapped in two, something deep inside my soul died. Any small fragment of hope I may have had for love in this hell house was finally shattered in that instant. The broken model car went out in the trash, and I actually snuck outside that night, tore a small hole in the bag and dug through the disgusting garbage and fished it out. I hid it in my room for a while and secretly tried to fix it, but it was bent and damaged beyond repair. Even if I had succeeded in repairing it, what would I have done then? I couldn't put it on a shelf, or anywhere it would be seen or she would go crazy. So I ended up eventually taking it to school with me and disposing of it there. It was like throwing away a dream. It was around this time, after I had tried running away from home and had the police force me to come back; after telling adults I thought could help about the abuse and having that backfire and result in severe consequences; that I came to the demoralizing realization that there was no escape. I would have to find a way to survive. I would have to endure. I would have to reach deep and find an unrelenting, defiant perseverance. It was in that moment that the fire was lit; the fire that would light the way through the seemingly endless dark days to come. Finding ways to persevere, to survive, to slide around trouble and to make it through unbearable times became my only hope. In fact, it became the very reason for living. I was not going to let this destroy me. I constantly reminded myself that I would not always be a trapped young boy, I would someday be a man, and I would be free, and that when the sun rose on that new day, I would never wake up afraid again. The days would turn to weeks, then months and then years, and I would rise from the ashes, climb the mountain of my dreams and reach the apex a victorious man having survived the long, long walk.

Not Alone
~ Friendship Pierces the Darkness ~

When you are a young boy, and abusive treatment becomes the norm in nearly every facet of your life, you can't help but to isolate yourself; emotionally and mentally curling up into the fetal position. As it seemed no place was safe, I turned inward, avoiding connection wherever I could. I kept to myself. I didn't talk to anyone I didn't have to. I found solace in being alone. I would hide in my room and quietly play the old classical acoustic guitar and ukulele my dad had given me, writing songs and composing music. I would draw pictures of cool cars or create abstracts with pens. The privacy issues of my bedroom made it difficult at times to hide away up there, so I would also spend lots of time alone in a place that had always welcomed me – the woods. There was a park on the edge of town that was only about 4 or 5 blocks away, and I went there by myself a lot. I would find a spot and just sit for hours, listening to the sounds of the trees and the birds. In them I could hear a symphony. It was living, breathing music, and I would lose myself in it. From my earliest years, I was never afraid of the natural world. I had an innate understanding of my connection to the earth and truly felt her as my Mother. That indigenous sense was always in me, always guiding me, and always a safe place to escape to. Those times alone taught me to enjoy my own company, and to not need to depend on others for my happiness. That was a gift. Such is the way with real gifts; sometimes you find them in the most unexpected places, and discover that you are not alone after all.

There was no greater friend to me during those years of abuse than my very own brother. From the goofy games we played in front of the mirror, to the ridiculous comedy skits we recorded on tape, and the silly comic strips we drew on paper, the laughter we found with each other was a saving grace. That sense of humor which Native people have always leaned on in seasons of struggle was fully activated in me and my brother in our time of need. And the elaborate make-believe *Batman & Robin* escapades, fake fight scenes, made-up pro football games and imaginary basketball leagues we created and enacted kept our minds distracted from the deranged hell we were living in. Together, we lit a small candle in the ominous darkness and found our way. My brother, my friend, you lifted me up when I was down. You fought for me when I could not fight. You spoke for me when I had no voice. No one could fathom all I have survived. But *you* can, because you were there, surviving it right beside me. Thank you my brother. You are my dearest friend, and I love you more than you could imagine.

My dad had always been an athlete, and a very good one. But his dreams of athletic success never came to fruition, and at 18-years-old he took a job at General Motors on the assembly line. My father made good money, but he never loved what he did, and many times, we heard that lament over dinner. Also, a fair amount of the money he made was spent on drinking and other addictions. My dad's father had been an amazing musician and had even had some nominal success before it all went away and his life was swallowed up by that old demon that has come calling for so many people of American Indian lineage – alcohol. As a result, I would never meet my paternal grandfather, as he died at age 38. My father was just 4 years old when his dad passed, and I believe he never fully healed from that loss. His mother (my grandmother) was eventually remarried and I cannot be sure, but I suspect that my grandmother did not necessarily encourage my father to give a music career a try. On the contrary, I always had the sense that as a result of her experiences with my grandfather, she had instilled in my dad the notion that pursuing a music career was not only risky, but irresponsible, and that it was more mature to seek a job that would provide a consistent, steady income. And so my dad settled, and sold his dreams for a weekly paycheck. I don't blame him for it, but my father's dinnertime laments convinced me that he had always secretly wanted more out of his life. I believe that desire was what kept my father involved with sports. It was a distraction that allowed him to use at least one of his gifts – athleticism.

He was a member of local basketball leagues, golf leagues, ping pong leagues, pool leagues, and softball leagues, and he had a wall of championship trophies to prove his athletic prowess. Softball became the sport that my dad would spend the most time at, and we spent a lot of summer weekends at a ballpark somewhere while my dad's team often played their way to yet another championship. It was during one of these weekend softball tournaments that I met him. His name was Kelly, and we were both about 10 years old. He was the eldest son of one of the players on my dad's team. I don't remember all the specifics, but the fact that I had long hair prompted Kelly to call me a girl that day, which brought back a terrible memory from a few years earlier. I have never been the fighting type, but on that day I found something that felt like courage within me and we ended up having the kind of fight 10 year old boys have, which wasn't much. Later that day, both our fathers found out about it, and made us apologize to each other, which we did, if begrudgingly so. Well, as the story goes, Kelly and I became the best of friends. He lived in another town, so he got to know me outside of the environment of perpetual torment I suffered every day at home and at school. He got to meet a version of me that almost nobody knew. He got to see the person that had always been there inside me, but had been driven into hiding by abuse and bullying. I usually saw Kelly during weekend softball tournaments, which were times of reprieve from

Emily's wrath, so I was happy. And I was very happy to finally have a friend. Sometimes I would get to stay the night at Kelly's house. I always loved that, but I was terrified every time I stayed that I would wet the bed, and that I would lose my friend. I don't recall ever wetting the bed at a sleepover at Kelly's house, but whether it happened or not, Kelly remains my best friend to this day. If he is reading this, I want to thank him for his lifelong friendship, and tell him that he could never know how much it has meant to me. I am so glad he decided to call this mixed-blood kid with the long hair a girl all those years ago!

Then there was Rick. Rick was a bit of nerdy kid who lived just a few blocks from me. I don't remember how we met, but we became fast friends through our love of comic strips. And the comic strips I speak of were our own creations, not the kind you buy. We drew them ourselves and had tablets full of them. I still have my tablets even now. Mine was called *The Kools* and his was called The *Loozoids*, and both were centered around a car that could do all kinds of amazing things like fly and drill through a hillside. We would both write each other's characters and cars into our own comic strip, and we had a lot of fun laughing and reading them with each other. When I was in my mid-teens I went to Rick's house one morning. As I sat in his kitchen that day I watched in awe as my friend whipped up an omelet for himself and for me. I was amazed by his total freedom to make his own breakfast. I felt so strange watching him have total run of that kitchen, the cupboards, the refrigerator and even the stove. Not to mention the fact that when he asked me if I wanted an omelet, I had to ask him what it was because I had never heard of such a thing. Rick was astounded by that, and thus began to ask me questions about my home life. When I told him some of what things were like, he actually called his mom into the kitchen so she could hear too. Their strong reactions to even the small bit I shared were like a loving hand reaching through what had become a thick fog of false normalcy. I had lost lucidity. Love and happiness had become distant, faded reflections, barely visible anymore. My eyes had lost their light, my soul, its hope. I was trapped in a haze of madness, fear and abuse. I could no longer see what was normal. I could no longer discern what was healthy and what was sick. A dark cloud had descended upon me, and I had forgotten what it was like to live in the sun, to dance in the fields and to be free. Rick and his mother reached through the shadows that day and helped me remember, helped me hear the music again off in the distance, and reminded me that I was not alone. After high school, Rick and I enlisted in the military together. We lost touch. I did my short military stint and got out. Rick did the same. I bumped into him one day in that old forgotten town, and he leaned into my car window and told me he was going back into the service, as he just could not find work in the civilian world. I wished him well and we each went on our way. It was the last time I would ever see Rick. He was killed in Iraq by a sniper's bullet. When I heard the news I went down into my studio closet, dug through my memory bag and pulled out my comic strip tablets, and read 'The Loozoids' through thick, hot tears as I remembered my childhood friend. Thank you, Rick. Thank you for reaching out to me, for being my friend, for imparting your courage, and for making me my very first omelet.

Then there was Donny. We became friends in Junior High. Donny never seemed to notice or be concerned with the things so many of the other kids in school bullied me about. He just liked me, and he was fun – crazy fun! With the help of his dad, Donny had fixed up a snazzy 68' Oldsmobile Cutlass, and at 16 was driving that car to school. I rode with him nearly every day, and it was a welcome reprieve from the school bus and the mean-spirited bullies that beat up on other kids while waiting at the bus stop. Donny was a breath of fresh air for a teenaged boy like me who was struggling to find his voice. He was wild as hell, and just a down to earth good person through and through. His friendship was like a beacon of light-hearted hope in the darkness. It made me feel good about myself again. I was likeable! I was fun! And even more amazing, I was even kind of cool! During the years right after high school, hanging out, chasing girls and racing cars with Donny was like a kind of intense therapy that began to heal my deeply damaged self-image. He was a great, great friend who showed me how to let loose and throw caution to the wind and have a good time. Donny came to visit me one summer not long ago with his beautiful wife and two teenage kids. We had a great time reminiscing. A short time later I received word that Donny had suddenly died. A massive heart attack on the fourth of July took my dear friend from his family, and from me. He was in his mid forties. I will never forget his smile, his laugh and his good nature. Thanks for the ride Donny. You could have never known how desperately I needed it.

Each of these friends imparted unique gifts to me, and their love drew me out of hiding, out of the darkness, and into the light. Their friendship helped to heal my broken heart, and saved me from despair. Though I had been forced into isolation, they found me and rescued my spirit. And yet, in my solitude I had also found my own essence. I saw myself in that quiet, lonely space, and decided that I was not so bad after all. And my time sitting on the brown bosom of Mother Earth as the winds kissed my cheek, the sunlight warmed my shoulders, the trees whispered their secrets and the birds sang to me their love, revealed the answer to a deep mystery – no matter how empty we are, how far away we may be, or how completely we have hidden our soul from the hurt, we are never, ever, alone.

Sweet, Sweet Rain
~ Tears of Heaven ~

I was 4 years old. It was dark and stormy outside, and I was in my undies looking out the window in awe. I was mesmerized by the power of the Wakinyan Tanka (thunder beings). It seemed their sacred energy was pouring into my spirit, and I felt a deep resonance with them to my core. I ran to the kitchen to ask Mumma if I could go outside. I can't explain it, but I was being drawn to what was out there, and I wanted to feel the rain on my skin. My mom said yes, and I ran out the door excitedly with her following behind. As she watched me from the covered porch, I danced and twirled as the heavenly droplets kissed my young face and soaked my body through and through. As the waters streamed down my small boyish chest and shoulders, I gazed up at the shadowy clouds, with arms outstretched, and for the first time in my young life, felt the divine connection to Father Sky and Mother Earth, and their love for me. It was sublime. I don't know that I have ever felt more alive than I did in that moment on that day, dancing nearly naked in the rain with my mother looking on with loving eyes at her firstborn son. Then it happened. Out of nowhere, a thunderbolt struck. The flash was so bright and the thunderclap so loud that it was like a bomb had gone off. I froze in terror, turning to look for my mother. I have never forgotten her face in that moment. She exuded pure tranquility. There was no fear. No worry. Only a relaxed motherly smile as she stood there in her flannel shirt, long dark hair loose and arms folded, watching. And I knew it was okay. I didn't have to be afraid. And so, with admittedly a bit more trepidation, I went back to twirling in the rain. I now know why I *needed* to go outside that day. There was a message out there waiting for me. The Wakinyan Tanka wanted me to know that a terrifying storm was coming. And that no matter how scary things might become, I only needed to look through the rains, and I would find a loving face, a loving heart, a loving place to reassure me that everything would be okay. To this day, I still have a strong aversion to sudden loud noises, so I have never been a big fan of fireworks, guns, or anything that startles unexpectedly with a loud bang. Thus, even the warnings of Spirit can sometimes leave a mark on one's soul. But the thunders have always been my friends, my messengers and my medicine. Because from the moment they kissed my face and soaked my body with their waters on that warm, stormy summer day so long ago, their power has never left me. Their rains wrapped my tender naked being in a loving blanket of knowing and connection. And thus I have always known that there would be a smile waiting for me on the other side of the storm.

Some of what I am going to reveal in this chapter will require courage for me to share, and will also test my limits as a writer as I try to navigate how to put into written words the sexual abuse I suffered in a way that is both honest, and yet maintains my personal dignity. At the end of the day, I must conclude that I am writing this book as much for the reader as I am for myself. And the purpose in sharing my story is to expose the sickness of abuse so healing may come. Ultimately, in order to shine a truthful, revealing light on sexual abuse, it is unavoidable that some information of a personal nature must be shared. Therefore, with healing being the motivation, I will endeavor to courageously impart the truth of my experience, safeguarding my privacy where I can, as I reveal what I must so that the sickness cannot hide in the shadows any longer.

Emily was a sexual deviant. From the start, she did and said things that were sexually inappropriate, invasive and perverse. From that moment in the bathtub when she disrespected my desire for privacy when I was 9 years old, the abnormal sexual behavior continued. There were more bathroom invasions. There were the numerous curiously timed, unannounced intrusions into my bedroom when I was in various states of undress. I can't count the number of times she caught me naked, never apologizing, but instead always acting as if I was overreacting when I would quickly hide myself. It was very strange, and very confusing to a growing boy. As I explained in a previous chapter, the bedroom I shared with my brother was not conducive to privacy to begin with, as our sisters' room was situated so that they could not even get out of their room without going through ours. So my sisters inevitably walked in on me when I was indecent on more than one occasion. But those instances were rare, and of course, never intentional. My sisters certainly couldn't change the way the house was built! And they almost always knocked on the inside of their own door before they opened it to see if the coast was clear. Even so, there were those entirely unintentional 'oops' moments, and they added to the overall sense of having absolutely no privacy. Emily, on the other hand, had an uncanny sense for barging into my room right when I was naked. And it happened far too often to be coincidental. To this day, I don't know how she knew when I was undressed, but I have my suspicions. It wasn't too long after we had moved in to that house with my dad and Emily that the physical abuse started. Emily's preference with me was to either slap my face, or force my pants and underwear down so she could spank my bare rear end with her hand. This was not 'corporal punishment'. My dad used a belt on my backside one time in his life, and I think it hurt him more than it did me. He never did it again. But what Emily regularly subjected me to was something more. It was disturbing. And it became obvious to me over time that she was just trying to see and touch my naked behind. She would concoct some off the wall reason that

I was in trouble, and you could almost see that her anger was feigned as she ordered me to drop my pants. And if I resisted at all, pleading with her not to do it, she would become physically aggressive, slap my face and then forcibly pull my underwear down and have her way with me. So from the time I was 9 until about 12 years old, that was the way things went. It was a regular regiment of sexually invasive behavior, along with all the mental, emotional and physical abuse. As time passed, I began to lose any sense of my right to privacy, as she perpetually invaded my personal space. It didn't happen every day, but it happened enough. Then, along came puberty.

Throughout all the years I lived and grew up in that house, Emily had made a habit of making overtly inappropriate sexual comments in the presence of me and my siblings. She constantly said things about my sister's anatomy that made me cringe. I felt so sorry for my sister. And there were other unseemly thoughts she would speak out loud. But all of those pale in comparison to the times she felt inclined to tell us about the size of my father's private parts. Never mind that I had already been made to shower with him, but no child should have to hear those things about their dad, much less see them. Decades later, at my father's funeral, Emily sat beside me and my aunt and told us that she wished she could sever my dad's penis and take it home with her. Yes, I know, it's horrifying, but she actually said it. And on that day my aunt got a small dose of the sexually twisted world I had grown up in.

Puberty began for me in my 12th year. One Sunday, my brother and I were taking our weekly shower together when I looked up to adjust the showerhead. To my utter bewilderment, I was stunned to see Emily looking over the wall at us with a camera, and I instinctively raised my hand to try and block the lens as she snapped a photo. The reason I so vividly remember my raised hand is because that picture is in one of Emily's photo albums. That's right, she actually had it developed. And I have seen it. I was only 13 years old. As it turned out, my raised hand wasn't enough to protect my privacy, as the photo captured all of my naked body from behind. Thankfully, my brother - and the other side of me - was concealed from view. Afterward, she acted like it was all in good fun, and completely normal for a step-mother to sneak in and take pictures of her teenage step-son in the shower. And, after 4 years of having my sexual privacy slowly stripped away, I found myself accepting her explanation for taking a nude photo of me. This is what happens to an abused child. You lose your sense of what is appropriate. Your 'right and wrong compass' no longer points the way, and you begin to doubt your own self-worth. Needless to say, weekly showers were not the same after that, as I spent a lot of time looking up so as to not be caught off guard again. But it turns out that was a futile effort, as I have since learned from my sister that Emily made a regular habit of slipping into the bathroom when my brother and I were in the shower. No place was sanctified. Not even in a bedroom or a bathroom could I conceal myself from her. A short time after that photo was developed I was alone in the house one summer day with Emily downstairs. I decided to go outside, and thus headed down to the first floor and toward the back door. Emily stopped me in the dining room with a peculiar look on her face and ordered me into the bathroom. I was terribly afraid of her, so I didn't dare disobey. Once I was in the bathroom she shut the door behind us. What she said next shocked me. She asked me if I had any pubic hair yet. I was speechless. I didn't know what to say, and I didn't know what to do. Reluctantly and sheepishly, I replied in a barely audible voice that I only had a little. She responded to that by folding her arms and demanding that I pull down my pants so she could "see how I was developing", also making mention of a comparison to my dad. My face flushed nervously and I suddenly felt warm all over and had the strangest mix of conflicting sensations I had ever experienced. My mind was feeling one thing but my 14 year old body was feeling another, and that sick realization mortified me and completely confused me into blaming myself for what was happening to me. And so I did as I was told, unfastened my pants and pulled them down along with my underwear. I went numb as I stood there, my genitals exposed to her leering eyes. After a minute or so of her looking me over, she finally left me alone in the bathroom. I was devastated. By coercing me into revealing my most private parts to her that day, Emily had succeeded in deeply damaging my natural, healthy sexuality by making me ashamed of it and twisting it into a self loathing mental bondage that would take many years to unravel. And that fact only served to embolden her. After that, the unwelcome advances and intrusions escalated as she managed time and again to catch me in awkward, embarrassing moments, always flashing that barely discernable, devious grin when she did. One day, when I was about 15, I was getting ready to head down the stairs; she was in her bedroom making the bed with the door open and said something to me. As the conversation ensued, she suddenly just took her t-shirt off for no apparent reason. She had no bra on, so all was revealed. When she saw my reaction, she quickly covered herself and weirdly made out like it was just a mindless accident. I am not sure what she was up to that day, but I have never 'accidentally' undressed in front of anyone, so I can only assume she took off her top intentionally. What she had in mind I'll never know, but it certainly fits the narrative of her warped sexual fixation on me.

I was 16. I had begun lifting weights, and for several years had been practicing a martial arts form called Aikido. I was becoming a young man. My muscles were growing and I was gaining a little confidence in myself, albeit gradually. It was another summer day, and I was heading out of the house for some teenage activity I no longer recall. She stopped me in the dining room, the same place she had stopped me when I was 14 to force me into the bathroom. On this day, she was angry about something. I sensed immediately that she had an ulterior motive. But something was different on this day. *I was different.* I resisted. Her response to my resistance was no surprise, as she ordered me to pull down my pants so she could spank me. And I said *no*. That's right. For the first time in my life, I said no to her. With that "no", I finally asserted that Emily could not violate me anymore, could not abuse me anymore, and could not invade my privacy anymore. Her reaction to my telling her "no" was to take a swing at me. Either my Aikido training or just my reflexes kicked in and I caught her hand before it reached my face. So she swung and tried to slap me with her other hand, and I caught that one too. So there I was with my arms crossed, my hands firmly gripping both her wrists, and I was suddenly very afraid. It had all happened so fast. My quick reflexes had gotten ahead of my fear, and now I was in a pickle. Emily's pale face was turning beat red as she pulled against my newfound strength. I was terrified to release her. And then a realization washed over me – *I was stronger than she was.* I was physically bigger and more powerful than her. That realization gave me the courage to tell her that I would let her go, but only on one condition: she would never hit me again. She just kept seething for me to let her go, but I kept insisting that she promise to not hit me anymore. As I held her in my grip, I saw something in her eyes I had never seen. She was afraid of me. I had a strange internal response to that – I actually felt sorry for her. That response was not because I was a transcended being of higher consciousness; it was because I was a victim of years of sadistic abuse. That is what abuse does. It affects your mind in ways you'd never believe unless you have experienced it yourself. Case in point; it can cause you to feel bad for a woman who was just attempting to sexually exploit and abuse you. Emily never agreed to stop hitting me that day, but I finally released her, expecting the worst. To my surprise, she just huffed and puffed on by me and left me there in stunned silence, catching my breath. The epic struggle that took place in the dining room that day was a baby-step toward my healing and freedom. To this day I am proud of myself for finally taking a stand in that moment. On that day, I became a man.

Decades later, as a happily married man with a successful music career and a lot of healing behind me, I found myself in my secluded studio in the mountains looking out the window once again in awe of a storm. And I felt the power of the Wakinyan Tanka calling to me, just as they had all those years ago when I was just a 4-year-old boy. So I took a break from what I was doing and headed for the door, but not before I undressed completely. As I stepped out into that warm, humid midsummer air, the rain began to fall. I walked out into it and looked up as I reached my arms for the heavens. The droplets kissed my face and danced on my skin as my tears joined the waters that streamed down my body. The thunders rumbled above, and I heard their message. I remembered their powerful warning, and my mother's smile. I remembered my boyish twirling in the rain. But most of all, I remembered how Father Sky and Mother Earth had known my tender naked being, and had loved me just as I was, inviting me to experience deep physical and spiritual connection; and I could feel them telling me that they loved me just the same today. As the pouring rains once again washed over me and soaked my skin, I felt the shame of sexual abuse that had imprisoned my sexuality and warped my body image for so long, slip away, and I felt myself letting go as I began to slowly turn and spin, my arms outstretched to the sky. I had come full circle. I was free. Finally free. Free to dream. Free to love myself. Free to say no. Free to fly. And free to dance. Yes, at long last I was free to dance in the sweet, sweet rain.

Runaway
~ Cries for Help ~

For most of the first 3 years that we lived with my dad and Emily there were biweekly weekend visits with our mom. Not long after Mumma had given custody to my father, she met and married another man. His name was Jon and he would be my mom's 3rd husband. He was a farmer, had long hair (which my mother always loved on a man) and a strong, sturdy build. He seemed like a nice enough guy, but I had been fooled before so I was very careful not to get too close to him at first. Just before that time, my mom had been the victim of a medical malpractice scheme. A doctor had falsely claimed she had a tumor in her throat and convinced her to have it surgically removed. During the procedure he made the mistake of slicing one of her vocal cords in half, rendering her speechless when she awakened. My mother had been a singer all her life, and had a beautiful voice. I have a recording of her singing that will one day end up on an album with me doing harmony vocals. Regardless, from that day forward, my mother never sang again, and I am convinced that she began to quietly die inside a little each day after that. For over a year, my mother couldn't speak, and had to write on notepads to communicate. After that, she decided to undergo a risky procedure to receive a

Teflon vocal cord. The surgery was a success, but it still took my mom months of voice therapy to learn to talk again. All of this resulted in a lawsuit that went on for years. Ultimately, Mumma settled and ended up with a pittance of what she would have received had she been able to go the distance. But she couldn't. Bills were piling up and my mom's nerves were shot, so she took the payoff. It wasn't a lot, but it was enough to get out of the red with collectors and buy herself a nice car. So when the weekend visits started, my mother was in a pretty good place. She had a good car, a respectable home and a new husband. And she could talk again. It was after about 2 years of living with my father, and during one of our weekend stays, that Mumma asked us how things were going at dad and Emily's home. I think she could sense that we were a little afraid to talk about it, so she assured us that we were safe to tell her the truth. And so we did. It was like a dam broke as we all poured out our hurts, and our mom sat wide-eyed as she heard firsthand about the horrible abuse her children were suffering. My mother was small in stature, but fearless in spirit. As she listened to us speak of our misery through our tear-filled eyes, I could see her getting angrier and angrier. I started to feel hopeful that my mom could make the abuse stop. After all, I had seen her do it before.

When we were still living with Mumma, before my dad met Emily, *he* was the one that had the 'every other weekend' visitations. And during that time-period, my father had a girlfriend named Mickey. I don't know where he found these women, but Mickey was an abuser too. While we were there visiting one weekend, she stormed into the bathroom while I was peeing, grabbed me by my hair and yanked me off my feet. I was only about 7 years old, so I was no match for this large, angry white woman. As she dragged me by my long hair across the linoleum bathroom floor and up the carpeted stairs yelling about how I looked like a girl, the movement caused my underwear to partly slide down and I ended up with bad carpet burns on my back and butt. Mickey dragged me into a bedroom and picked me up and threw me onto the bed, after which she aggressively pulled off my underwear and tossed them out the door onto the hallway floor. As I cried, she screamed at me to stay in that bed and not come out until she told me to. She then left the room, slamming the door behind her. I cried and cried, all alone in that dimly lit room. I had no idea what I had done to deserve such treatment. It was the first time I had ever experienced that kind of abuse, and it tore me apart. A short time later, I heard someone coming up the steps. The door swung open. It was Mickey, and she was still visibly furious. "Why are you still crying boy?" she snarled as she approached me. I was terrified. She jerked the blankets away from me, and snapped at me to hold out my arms. So there I was, just a small boy, naked and trembling on my knees in the center of that big bed, tears in my eyes and arms held out in front of me, not knowing what was next. For reasons I still cannot fathom, Mickey began to dig her nails into my little arms, scratching me deep, over and over. I wailed in pain, but she kept clawing at me. When I reactively tried to pull my arms away, she slapped my face and made me extend them again. It was all so terrifying and surreal. When she finished scratching my arms she left again. I fell over helplessly onto my side on the bed and sobbed uncontrollably for some time. A while later a teenaged girl I never saw before came into the room and brought me my clothes and told me I could come out. I got dressed and nervously descended the stairs, eyes swollen from crying. Mickey had left the apartment. I was safe, for now at least. When I went home after that weekend I told Mumma what had happened and showed her my terribly scratched up arms and the carpet burns on my backside. Two weeks later my mom drove us to dad and Mickey's place for our regular visit, but when we got there she made us wait in the car as she went and knocked on the door. Mickey came outside, and my petite Lakota Ina (mother) proceeded to dress her down. Mickey was much larger, but Mumma was fearless as she pointed her finger in that big white woman's face. I heard words come out of my mother's mouth I had never heard her utter before. She threatened the life of that nasty woman that day. Once she finished with Mickey, my mom came and opened the back door of the car. She assured me not to worry, and that Mickey would not touch me. I was encouraged, but still afraid as Mumma drove away that day. But whatever my mom threatened that woman with that afternoon must have done the trick, because she never said a cross word nor laid a hand on me ever again.

And so it was that I found reason to believe in Mumma's motherly powers. She had made it stop before; maybe she could do it again. What I could not comprehend at age 12 was that because my mother had voluntarily surrendered physical custody to my dad and Emily, it was nearly impossible that she could ever regain it. Not to mention that she did not want to do anything to jeopardize her weekend visits with us. When the Mickey incident happened years earlier, my mother was the one in the driver's seat. She had custody, and therefore, the power. That was no longer the case, and I was too young and naïve to realize it. So I informed my mother privately that weekend that I was going to run away and come to live with her. What could she say? Her son wanted to live with her. And he was being terribly abused. Thus my mom didn't have the heart to turn me away. And the truth was, she didn't really believe I would do it. After all, I was only a boy and she lived more than 10 miles away from my dad and Emily. But my mom *did* want to act. She even made mention of seeing an attorney. Her children were suffering, but she was truly between a rock and a hard place. What she didn't know, was that my plan to run away was not just 12-year-old bluster. I was serious.

And when my mom and Jon drove us home that Sunday afternoon, I was paying attention to the roads, making a mental map of how I would make my escape.

It was early Monday morning. I had been awake most of the night nervously contemplating my plan. When I quietly slid out of bed in the dark and proceeded to get dressed, I was overcome with two emotions; fear and sadness. I was afraid for the obvious reason that I was about to run away from home. But the sadness was an emotion I hadn't expected. By running away, I was leaving my brother and sisters. I was the oldest, and I felt like I was betraying them and leaving them vulnerable. I loved them, and I had a sense of responsibility for their well-being. And so I told myself that if I succeeded in escaping this hellish prison, maybe they could be set free too. Exiting the house without being detected was nerve wracking, but I finally slipped out the back door, unlocked the padlock to the garage, got on my bike and rode away. Playing my mental map in reverse, I pedaled down sidewalks, then streets and then roads out of town. At first it was dark. But then the sun began to rise over an open field as I rode my cherished bicycle down that blacktop country road, and felt freer than I had felt in a long, long time. Thoughts of my siblings waking up and discovering I was gone troubled me, but I pressed on, choosing instead to focus on how liberating it was to feel the open wind on my face. 10 miles is a long way to go on a bike, especially one without gears. But I was a determined young boy, and I couldn't wait to see my mother's face when I showed up at her door. It was an odd feeling to ride my bike up the driveway of my mom and Jon's home that morning, being that we had just been there the day before. The sun was well above the horizon as I knocked on the door and waited. When Mumma came and looked through the window, she could not conceal her shock. She opened the door and immediately told me that she never believed I would really do it as she hugged me and welcomed me inside. Jon was there, and he and my mom spoke openly about what they should do. It was clear to me from their tone that what I had done was serious, and they wanted to support me however they could. So Mumma instructed me to hide my bike in the cornfield behind the house. After that, she and Jon sat with me and explained what they were expecting to happen. They told me that they could not legally keep me, but that they would do whatever they could without breaking the law. It was painful to hear that, on so many levels. Jon had some farm chores to do, but he told Mumma to let him know if anyone called and that he would keep watch on the road. Well, it wasn't long before the phone rang. It was my dad on the line asking if I was there. Mumma had to tell him yes. After she hung up she told me that my dad was coming for me. I was adamant; I was *not* leaving. Jon told me that if my dad showed up without a warrant, he would not let him take me against my will. A short time later I heard a car in the driveway and peeked out the window to see. It was my dad. Jon met him at the door and asked if he had a warrant, strongly asserting that he wasn't letting me go without one. A few moments later I saw my dad walking back to his car looking small and defeated. It broke my heart to see him like that. It was never my intention to hurt him, or my brother and sisters. I loved my dad; I just couldn't live in misery any longer. I had to *do* something about it, so I ran. As I watched him drive off, I wondered if that would be it. I wondered if maybe I would be allowed to stay with my mom. But Jon told me I needed to prepare myself because if my dad returned it would be with a warrant, and he would have no choice but to hand me over. So I went upstairs to a bedroom and began watching out the window. It wasn't long before I spotted my father's car coming down the road again with a police car behind him. I snuck out of the bedroom and down the stairs to watch the front door. When the police came to the door asking for me, Jon stood on the other side with his hand on a shotgun and demanded to see a warrant. When I saw the paper, I slipped quietly back up the stairs and into the bedroom, locking myself inside. As I peeked out the window, I was horrified to see that my dad had brought Emily and my brother and sisters with him. I couldn't believe he had brought Emily along. What was he thinking? Did he not know why I ran away? Now I was even more afraid, and determined not to be taken. A few minutes later Jon knocked at the bedroom door and told me I had to go. I didn't make a sound, and after a couple more attempts I heard his footfalls head back down the stairs. Then there were more footsteps, and a strange man began speaking. It was the police officer. Again, I was as still as a mouse. Then he gave up and went back downstairs. A bit of time passed, and I began to wonder what was happening. Then I heard Mumma's soft voice at the door, calling my name with such concern that I approached and responded. It was my mother who convinced me I had to go that day. She promised me she would look into what could be done about me coming to live with her. I finally opened the door and Mumma took me in her arms and held me, before leading me down the stairs and handing me over to my dad. I can't imagine how hard that had to be for her. I had to go and retrieve my bike from the cornfield. My dad had bought that bike for me, and it was utterly humiliating to have to bring it to him so he could put it in the trunk. As I got into the back seat of the car, my brother and sisters' faces were like masks. Emily didn't say a word, and neither did my father. That ride home was the longest 10 miles of my life.

Not long after, my father took us to see The Friend of the Court. He made it crystal clear what I was to say: that I did not want to have weekend visitations with my mother any more. There was no way I was going to cross him, and so I forced myself to say it. And that was it. The biweekly weekend visits with Mumma stopped. We were not allowed to see her; ever. One day

I was riding my bike down the sidewalk in town and noticed a car beside me on the street traveling at about the same speed I was. I glanced over and saw Mumma looking back at me from the passenger side of the car. Jon was driving. I jumped off my bike and ran to her. She hugged me through the window with tears in her eyes and told me how much she missed me. We spent a few precious minutes together, and she made me promise not to say anything about seeing her. I never did. My father made some bad choices in his life, but that one stands atop them all for me. Forcing me to lie in a court setting about wanting to see my own mother to either teach my mom a lesson or protect himself from a custody battle was a despicable thing to do. My dad knew what Emily was doing to his kids, yet time and time again he just buried his head in the sand rather than face it. I guess it was too hard to think about another divorce, and easier to drown his conscience in the bottle while his children suffered at the hands of a monster. I don't remember if it was a year, or two, or three, but at some point our weekend visitations with Mumma resumed. Never again did I think of running away. But I never regretted that I did.

I still have that bike that I ran away with. I keep it like a trophy. It is a symbol of my courage to do the right thing even when it is painful and hard. When I got on that bicycle that morning and rode away from that house of horrors I made a powerful statement; the abuse being inflicted on me was *not acceptable*. From the seat of that bike I took a stand. That morning of liberation became a seed of hope for me that I carried until I was finally set free. So no matter how oppressive the darkness is, courage is always stronger. Rise up and claim your right to be in the light. Get on your bike and ride. And know that it is a great honor to bear the title, of *runaway*.

Love Will Find You
~ Light Overcomes Darkness ~

There are moments in this life that test your faith; moments when it seems love has left us and we are alone. Love is like the wind, sometimes it swirls and gusts, and you know it is present. But other times it is so still you can barely feel it, and yet it is all around you. We cry out for it and hear nothing, causing us to doubt its presence and question its existence. Love is a mystery. Its purpose is deep, and its vision long. We cannot always comprehend its hidden medicine. Thus, we must quiet our heart and lean in to hear its still, small voice. For just when it feels as if love has abandoned you and all hope is lost, it reveals itself, and you realize love has been with you all along.

I will never know what it was that came between my mother and father, but I know this; my dad never wanted to go through a divorce again. So when he married Emily, I believe he had made up his mind that he was going to make *this* marriage work, no matter what. Maybe that explains some of why my dad handled things with Emily the way he did. Perhaps he just didn't want to see his life upended again. Or it could be that he was just not courageous enough to face what was happening, and chose instead to live in quiet desperation and denial, using alcohol and drugs to escape the reality that his 2nd wife was abusing his children and that he was complicit in that abuse by allowing it to continue. All of that is, of course, just conjecture because he never divulged anything to me before he died so I am left to draw my own conclusions. I can tell you this; my father took abuse from Emily too. I know this because I witnessed it. One night my dad went to get some things from the store for Emily. When he returned and came through the back door into the kitchen, she hastily reached into the brown paper grocery sack and began fishing around for something specific. As it turned out, my dad had bought the wrong item, and Emily went ballistic. She began to violently slap and hit my father, who was backed into a corner and still holding the grocery bag as he made a futile effort to fend her off. I can still remember the timid, frightened tone of my dad's voice as he pleaded with her to stop hitting him. I had never seen or heard him like that. My father was supposed to be the focal point for my masculine identity. As a boy, I looked to him as a symbol of strength, and that night in the kitchen he had seemed so helpless; so weak. I felt so sorry for my dad. I can't imagine how he must have felt about being slapped around by his wife in front of his children. It had to have been humiliating. My dad was a quiet, gentle, soft spoken man, so he could be hard to read. And sometimes it seemed he didn't care about what Emily was doing to his kids. But I know, despite his struggles and shortcomings, my dad loved us and wanted to do right by us. And I will always hold in my heart the memories of those shining moments when he tried.

I was 11. It was a partly sunny afternoon and something was happening upstairs in dad and Emily's room – something loud and angry. They were fighting. The yelling and screaming could be heard even outside. After the shouting, came the slamming door. I watched from the back yard as Emily stormed out of the house, suitcases in hand, tossed them in the car, got in and drove away. I stood there stunned. Was that it? Was she gone for good? Maybe the nightmare was over! A few moments later my dad came out the back door and leaned forward reflectively, resting his arms on the wrought iron porch railing. I approached cautiously and quietly joined him. As the sun cast its warm, late afternoon glow on father and son, he spoke. Almost as if to himself, he said that if Emily did not come home that night, he would never let her come back again. Those words rang in my ears and went through my 11-year-old body like a sonic wave. As the sun went behind a cloud, my dad went back into the house, leaving me alone with my thoughts, and I found myself feeling more hopeful than I had in years. I looked up to the sky and prayed. All I had ever known about the spiritual life I had learned in the woods on my own, and from the subtle, day to day life lessons of indigenous ways I had grown up with. So I leaned into those understandings as I opened up my mouth and my heart and asked Wakantanka/God to please keep Emily from coming back home that night. I had never asked Spirit for anything before. It was just not my nature to pray that way. I always prayed for others, which it turns out is another indigenous trait. But on that day I prayed fervently for myself, begging for a spiritual intervention to save me from the hell I had been living in. At the conclusion of my prayer, the sun began to break through the clouds, and the God fingers appeared, the beams of light illuminating my young face. It felt like a sign; like an answer. But my hope was dashed that night, as the headlights of Emily's car pulled into the driveway and chased away my visions of a new life without her. I was crushed. Did I not pray right? Did God/Spirit/Wakantanka not hear me? Was God even real? If God was real, how could the desperate prayers of an 11-year-old boy, begging to be freed from his abusive tormentor, not be heard? And so I lost my faith that night. It would be decades before it would find me again.

My dad let Emily back into our life when she returned that evening, and everything stayed the same. The physical, mental, emotional and sexual abuse continued like nothing had happened. I don't know what my dad and Emily fought about that day up in their bedroom, but I now suspect it was about how she was treating his children. My reason for that hunch is because of what happened one night in the dining room. My siblings and I were all present when our dad and Emily began having an argument. Things began to escalate and my normally docile father's voice began to grow loud and angry. All four of us kids made an unspoken collective decision to head upstairs so they could have it out. But my dad told us to stay because he wanted us to hear what he had to say. So we eased awkwardly back toward the dining room, and quietly watched and listened as, for the first time, our father took Emily to task about how she was mistreating his children. With a roaring voice he yelled at her as she sat in stunned silence, demanding to know "why do you hate my kids?!!" He followed that by reminding her that she had told him many times how much she despised his children, and that if she hated them so much she was free to leave. There was no response from her, which seemed to enrage my dad even more. He slammed his fist onto the floor and it felt like it shook the whole house. He had tears in his eyes as he loudly unveiled his hidden feelings and demanded an answer from her. I had never seen my father so angry. It made me incredibly nervous, but I was so glad he was finally standing up for us. Emily was visibly shaken by my dad's rage, but I don't recall her ever uttering a word or making a sound. My dad finally gave us the okay to go upstairs to our rooms. As I lay in bed that night unable to sleep, a mix of emotions swirled inside me. On the one hand I was elated that my dad had finally called Emily out. It did me good to see the woman who had terrorized me sit there in that chair afraid. I was also flirting with a tenuous hope that she might actually decide to pack her bags and leave. On the other hand I was seriously worried about what would happen when my dad was back at work and we were again alone with Emily. I eventually fell into a fitful sleep. Well, Emily never moved out. But for a short time after that night, she was on her best behavior with us. It was bizarre to have her be so nice during that period. All the usual demented house rules still applied, but the overt abuse subsided. I walked on eggshells the entire time. And little by little, she slipped back into her old patterns until things ultimately returned to what they had been before that night in the dining room. My dad never took a stand like that again that am aware of. But seeing how he really felt that night about Emily's abusive behavior toward me and my brother and sisters did at least two things for me: it demonstrated his love for us and that – despite Emily's hate – we were deserving of that love.

I'll never forget *The Golden Band-Aid*. That was my dad's moniker for his metallic gold 1970 4-door Oldsmobile Delta 88. It was in that rusty, trusty car with the rumbling thrush mufflers that we all went to the Cedar Point amusement park one summer – *without* Emily. Aside from softball tournaments, we almost never went on family outings. That trip was one of the only times I remember us all having our dad to ourselves for a weekend, and it was like being released from prison. I had one of the best times of my entire childhood. Cedar Point was in northern Ohio, so it was a bit of a trip. It was also one of only 2 times before I was 18 that I would ever travel out of Michigan. The sun was shining as we rolled down the road in that old car, listening to music with our father behind the wheel seeming a bit like a kid playing hooky from school. It was getting near midday when my dad asked us all if we were hungry. Of course we were. We were *always* hungry. So he told my sister to hand him the bag of bologna sandwiches Emily had sent along. All we ever got to eat were those damn bologna sandwiches, which I had grown to hate, and it looked like today would be no different. So my sister handed the bag to my dad from the back seat, and I quietly resigned myself to eating the same awful lunch I was forced to eat nearly every day during our summer breaks from school. What my dad did next is one of my all-time favorite memories – he rolled down his window and tossed the whole bag out! We were astonished, and couldn't wipe the grins from our faces. Without having uttered a word, my father's act of compassion and understanding spoke volumes. After throwing out the sandwiches he told us to name whatever it was that we really wanted to eat and that, no matter what, he would get it for us. We could have asked my dad for filet mignon that day – never mind that none of us even knew what that was – and he would have treated us to it. But it was unanimous; of all the food choices we could have opted for, what we all wanted, was *SpaghettiOs*. And that night my dad gave us just that; in a skillet over a fire at our campsite, and we all stuffed ourselves like we hadn't in years. It was wonderful. I still love *SpaghettiOs* to this day for that very reason. We had the best time at Cedar Point the next day. I don't recall ever having that much fun with our dad before or since. The drive back home the following morning was mostly quiet. We all knew our brief respite was over, and a soft sadness hung in the air. But I looked out the open window in the back seat of *The Golden Band-Aid*, the wind and sun on my face, and ever so slightly, I smiled. *I was loved.* If even for just a moment, I got to frolic in the light, and revel in the knowing.

Love is always there, right under the surface. It sometimes hides its face from us like the sun behind a dark cloud, but it remains. And those fleeting moments that always seem to arrive just when we are about to give up all hope, are the saving grace that lifts us just enough to keep going. Love is like the drops of rain that wear away a great stone; it takes its time, and often shows itself in unexpected ways and places. I glimpsed it in my father's fist on the dining room floor, and when he tossed those bologna sandwiches out the window. That was love. So, no matter how far away it seems; or how far you've had to run to survive. And no matter how distant the memories have become, or how lost you may feel… love has always known. Love never left. And love – pure, gentle love – *will find you.*

I Am
~ Finding Your Voice ~

In Lakota spirituality we have an old custom called Hanblecheya – to cry for a vision – in which we go to a sacred place, deprived of food, water and clothing for several days and nights. We do this to beseech Tunkasila to give us a sign which will help us find our way on the good red road. It remains today a very important ceremonial tradition, because in our worldview there is nothing that matters more in this life than finding your purpose, your vision and your voice.

Summers were brutal in that house. Our rooms were upstairs and there was no air conditioning. That was the norm for a lot of people in those days. The difference for us was that Emily wouldn't let us open windows. *She* could do it, but we were not allowed. Add to that the rule about not being able to plug in anything electric and you can deduct that we were not allowed to use a fan. All those factors served to make our rooms into hotboxes during the dog days of summer. At times it became almost unbearable. It was on one of those wicked hot nights that Emily demonstrated just how sadistic her behavior could be. In my sisters' room, there was a window on the back wall near the corner. In that corner, adjacent to the window, there was a vertical register near the floor on the baseboard that was attached to another baseboard register on the other side of the wall, inside the closet in dad and Emily's room. In other words, if you got down on the floor and shined a light into either register, you could see all the way through to the other side. And again, the register was right by the window in my sisters' room. I can't imagine how hot it was that night, but I was having a hard time sleeping because of it. My physical makeup is such that I almost never perspire. These days I often joke that I am a desert rat! I have always been able to take the heat. But I was sweating that night. That upstairs bedroom was positively boiling. I don't recall the exact time it happened, but I do remember it being really late, like 3 or 4 in the morning. I think I had drifted off to sleep a bit, because I remember waking up suddenly as the door to my bedroom loudly flung open. It was Emily, and she immediately went into my sisters' room. Seconds later I heard the slapping start, and the crying. As I sit here writing, I can still hear the sickening sound of that monstrous woman beating my sister. Over and over and over Emily slapped her in the darkness, and with each crack of her hands on my sister's skin I felt more and more like a coward. I was her big brother, and I couldn't protect her. I wish I would have jumped out of my bed that night, ran into that room and assaulted that crazy woman. But I was paralyzed and silenced by fear. That is what abuse does to you. It traps you as much mentally as it does physically. And so it was, I was once again unable to help the same sister I had witnessed being molested years earlier. I felt like a failure. When Emily finished smacking and hitting my sister, she stomped out, slamming both bedroom doors behind her. The silent terror hung in the air like a dark fog, the only audible sound – the muffled sobs of my little sister on the other side of that door. I wanted so bad to go to her; to hold her. To tell her how sorry I was. But fear prevented me that act of kindness. The next day, my sister told me what had happened. She too, had been burning up that night, so she had slipped out of bed and quietly slid her window open to try and get some air. She had sat on the floor in that corner and rested her head on the wooden window sill. Emily had rushed in and beat her that night for opening that window. At first, we couldn't fathom how Emily knew, but it didn't take long for us to come to the jaw-dropping realization that there was only one way she could've known that my sister was sitting by her window that night. Emily had gotten up at that late hour, crawled into her closet on the floor and looked through that baseboard register. That was the only way she could have known, and it spoke volumes about just how deeply disturbed she was. During my sister's teen years, she wanted to use a curling iron, like any girl her age, for her arrow-straight hair. The problem again was that Emily forbade us to use anything that had to be plugged in. And so a battle ensued. My sister would sneak a curling iron into her room and get away with it for a while. Emily would find out, punish her and confiscate it, and within days my sister would have another one. This cycle went on for years. I'll never know where my little sister got all those curling irons, but her brave resistance was a gift that helped me find my own courage. And her decision to get up and open her window on that sweltering hot night showed me that she valued herself, and that I should value myself too. We *mattered*. We *counted*. And we deserved to be loved. Thank you my sister; for helping me to find my voice. I am who I am today in part because of your courage.

I'll never forget the day Emily was almost killed. We were all in the car heading somewhere. My dad was driving. Emily was a bit of a scavenger, always looking for freebies wherever she could find them. On that day, she spotted a burlap sack lying on the other side of the road, and made my dad pull over so she could get it. So, he pulled off the two-lane highway and Emily got out. She walked around the front of the car and was about to step onto the roadway when she saw a tractor-trailer. Emily lost her balance, and teetered precariously on her toes trying not to fall forward as that semi blew past just inches from her. She managed to stay on her feet, turned and gave my dad a 'whew, that was close' look, and then went and got the burlap sack. In that instant, a shocking thought entered my young mind – I was disappointed that she didn't get run over by that truck. That realization deeply disturbed me and made me feel like a bad person for having such a horrible thought.

But I understand it now. When you are trapped in the sick world of an abuser, you just want to escape, and it doesn't matter how. It would have been an awful thing to see, if Emily had been killed that way. I had no desire to see her perish like that. But the simple truth is, had she met her death that day, the abuse would have stopped, which would have been wonderful for me. And that is the chilling reality that sometimes causes victims of abuse to resort to violence. I once even had a fleeting thought about shooting her with the 20-gauge shotgun my dad had given me for hunting. It was never a serious consideration, but it did cross my mind that one time. The point is, I was not an evil person, but Emily *was*. And those thoughts about her possible demise were not because there was something wrong with me. They were an internal assertion that I deserved better, and the first whispers of a sound I had almost never heard before – my own voice.

My dad wouldn't let me get my driver's license until I turned 18, and I didn't get a car of my own until I graduated from high school. I took about half the money from my open house and bought a slightly rusty – but still very cool and super-fast – 1972 Chevelle for $350. I bought it from a mechanic who had done some of his magic with the engine, and warned me before I drove away to be careful with all that horsepower. It was in that car that I rebuilt a lot of my severely damaged self-esteem. With my boyhood pal Donny in tow, we went to town and won every back-road drag race we ran. Like I said, that Chevelle was fast. It was so fast, that during one summer I had beaten nearly every guy in town who had a car worth racing. I never lost a race. I was becoming a bit of a legend! I loved that car. After all, it was a lot like me – it needed some work but what was under the hood was incredibly strong. Behind the wheel of that wicked fast automobile I was *somebody*. Girls thought I was cute and guys thought I was cool, and that was almost like a drug for a young man who had never had either. Speaking of drugs, I should tell you that I never touched them – *ever*. In fact, I have never even taken a single hit from a cigarette. I did get drunk once, and after experiencing the feeling of losing control that night – and my cookies the next morning – I never did that again either. So, my drug was fast cars. Oh, and girls (I was 18 after all!). Every weekend Donny and I would roll into that neighboring town to 'cruise the pits'. 'The pits' were where the action was for our generation. On Saturday nights, there would be literally hundreds of cars, bumper-to-bumper, idling their way around two or three city blocks, all of us chatting or flirting as our vehicles slowly passed by one another. Other than the gals, the thing you had to really keep your eye on was your water temperature! This was long before computers and smart phones. If you wanted to 'add a friend' or 'like' a girl, you had to go out and meet them in person! My Chevelle had a menacing, rumbling cadence at an idle, and it would roar like a lion when I hammered the accelerator. That awesome sound was a release for my pent-up emotion. For 12 agonizing years, I had suffered cruelty in silence. I had been treated like garbage by abusive adults, many of my schoolmates and even a few of my teachers. But now, with my foot to the floor, I was the master of all that power, and I had something to prove. One night, long after the cruising was over and everyone had gone home, I was in my car alone on the east side of town, heading west. It had to be about 4 in the morning, because the streets were empty. As I rolled toward the city that night, the deep hurt I had suppressed for so long suddenly rose to the surface out of nowhere, and the blinding pain of all that emotion forced the gas pedal down. Approaching traffic lights at a lightning quick pace, I decided not to stop, no matter what happened. Faster and faster I raced like a bullet through blinking lights and into the center of town. Screaming at over 100 mph, the thunderous roar of my Chevelle echoed off the tall buildings as I blazed through one red light after another. I never stopped. All told, I ran 4 red lights that night, and kept the accelerator floored all the way to the railroad tracks on the far west outskirts of town. When I hit those tracks, my front right tire exploded. I could barely hold onto the wheel as I fought to keep from losing control of my car and rolling over, which would have meant almost certain death. Somehow, I kept that Chevelle from flipping and pulled off to the roadside. As I sat there catching my breath, that powerful engine emitted a deep rumble from under the hood as if to say "don't worry, I won't fail you". I then remembered that I did not have a spare. I knew I couldn't afford a tow truck, so after inspecting the damage, I decided I had no choice but to drive it home. And so it was that as my Chevelle and I limped along at a snail's pace on the side of the road with 8 miles to go, I finally let go and wept. The deep sobs wracked my body as years of hurt, pain and rage poured out of me. The roar of that car had been my internal scream – I had held it all inside for so long. And that blistering run through town had been a kind of spiritual catharsis. The loud, thunderous sound of that engine echoing off those buildings was my newfound voice, yelling in the face everyone that had ever abused me. I would never obey the warped rules of their red stoplights or speed-limits again. I risked it all that night. I cheated death. And as I painstakingly inched toward home on the side of the road in my wounded Chevelle, an odd happiness came over me. God had spared me, and there had to be a reason. The *next* 12 years would reveal that.

Political prisoner and Nobel Peace Prize nominee Leonard Peltier wrote a book entitled *My Life is My Sun Dance*. That title makes a parallel between the anguish of his lifetime of wrongful imprisonment and the suffering experienced at another of our sacred ceremonies, the Wiwanyang Wacipi – Sun Dance. For *my* story, the title could be *My Life is My Vision Quest*, as so many experiences have taken me to the mountain alone, depriving me of life's most basic needs. Years of crying, abuse and isolation rendered me nearly mute. I could barely whisper or even comprehend the notion that I mattered or had a reason for being here on this earth. But over time I found answers in that quiet solitary suffering, and release in the roaring thunder. On occasion, the light had pierced the darkness with visions and signs that pointed the way. And in an ironic twist, even the shadows illuminated my own strength. I found my endurance in the long walk, and my courage in the place of fear. Life has taken me to the high place of perspective, and forever changed me. No longer am I shortsighted. I can see for miles. And that vision has given me a voice – a voice to soothe, to proclaim and to shout. I have looked death in the face, and I am still here. I have peered into the darkness, and I am no longer afraid. I am strong. I am free. I am love. I am me. I am. *I am.*

Knowing
~ Consciousness Awakens ~

It is said, *to thy own self be true*. There is wisdom in that old adage. And yet, it is not as simple as it sounds, especially for a victim of child abuse. What I have told you about my childhood to this point is only a small sampling, an excerpt if you will, of everything I endured and survived. To tell every horrible tale would be too depressing and take too many books. You see, the thing about the abuse I experienced along with my siblings is that it was *hidden*. Almost nobody knew. A casual passerby might have seen kids playing in the yard and noticed the pretty curtains in the window and thought nothing was amiss. There were no black eyes or bruises for anyone to see. It was even concealed from our relatives and friends – mostly. I had a couple aunts and cousins who had seen enough to know that something was wrong, and I had told a few friends a little. But nobody did anything about it – except my maternal grandmother. She did inform the Child Protective Services agency, and an inquiry was made but nothing ever came of it. Suffice it to say, our abuse was perfectly disguised. Yes, the curtains looked nice from the outside. But on the other side of that window was a twisted monster whose hateful treatment toward us was deviously subtle and systemic. And after just a few years of being subjected to a daily regimen of warped rules, sadistic punishments and disgusting sexual behavior, the psychological damage was complete. I could no longer discern what was normal and what was not. The extent of the abuse was so all-encompassing that it had infiltrated every fiber of my being, and it was almost impossible to get my head around the enormity of it. This is why I have taken so long to write this book. It has taken decades of self-examination and healing to see it all, and even now some of the hurt remains. I have had to wipe away more than a few tears as I was writing some of this down because it stirred up such deep-seated emotion in me. Those scars fade with time, but they are always there. And there are a lot of them. This book cannot possibly tell it all. There was the time Emily threw my brother's carefully organized sports card collection all over the room as he stood there helpless and terrified, begging her to stop. There were all those days she locked us out of the house – even in the winter. We went to the park sometimes on those winter lockout days and built a fire to stay warm. And then there was that time I was suspended from high school for a day because I had been caught stealing, and I went to school anyway. The principle found out and ordered me off school grounds, never wondering why a teenaged boy would choose to come to school versus stay home for a day. He never knew the hell he was sending me back to. The high school was out in the country, so I walked those long roads back toward our house in town that day, and stayed away until school got out, never uttering a word about being suspended. Finally, there are the countless stories of terrible abuse my siblings could share. I hope they do someday. I want to say here how proud I am of my brother and sisters. They are all my heroes. All are wonderful parents and genuinely good people. None of us became alcoholics or drug addicts, nor have any of us ever abused a child. Each of us, in our own way, rose up victorious over our traumatic childhood. Regarding that childhood, all cannot be told here, but I have endeavored to impart enough to illustrate how utterly and completely devastating it was. Now I turn the page and begin the next chapter; the revealing process that comes after survival – *healing*. 'To thy own self be true'… yes indeed. But a victim of child abuse cannot even fathom that, until they make the incredible, enlightening journey of rediscovering their own true self.

I took an IQ test a few years back on a whim. When I was in elementary school I had to attend special education for mathematics at the same time I was reading at a collegiate level. The disparity between the two was puzzling. I was made to feel stupid by some of the 'popular' kids in school for being in that special education class. As it turned out, the difficulty I had with math was not because I wasn't intelligent enough to comprehend it, but was a direct result of the numerous times I had switched schools when I lived with my mother. I had simply slipped through the cracks. Once a teacher finally realized that when I was in 6th grade and brought me an abacus, it was like a dam broke, and I suddenly understood math. I had some serious catching up to do, and by the time I reached high school I was taking algebra. But the stigma of being called stupid stuck with me, and I had a low opinion of my intellectual aptitude because of it. As a result, Cs and Ds made regular appearances on my report cards, and I barely graduated from high school. Believe it or not, it was a creative writing class that nearly cost me my diploma! So, when I took that IQ test a few years ago I wasn't expecting much. You can imagine my surprise when I scored a 138. Not only was I not stupid, I was very, very smart! I often wonder what my grades would have been like had my home life (and my school life) not been so consumed by abuse. I'll never know the answer to that. And so I graduated. But what was I to do next? What did I want to be? Who was I? I hadn't a clue.

Going to college was never even on the radar for me. It was never discussed at home, and even when it did come up at school it never seemed realistic in my mind. The idea of college was so far-fetched that I rarely gave it any thought. Even if I *had* considered it, I would not have had the first clue how to proceed. I had no money or parental support, so I would have needed grants or financial aid, and I didn't have the first clue how to go about any of that. Thus, I never went to college. I had always dreamed of being a recording artist and having a music career, but I had no idea how to make that happen either. So I got a job at a department store shortly after graduating, and I made nowhere near enough money to move out. So, inconceivable as it was, I had no choice but to stay in that house where all the abuse still permeated everything. After that first wild summer of racing and chasing girls in my Chevelle, I did what a lot of desperate young men with limited options do: I enlisted in the military. And so the sensitive boy who couldn't harm an ant went off to learn how to kill people. I was 19-years-old. My stint in the service was short, and though I turned out to be quite a good soldier, it became clear to me early on that military life was not for me. I'll never forget the day they shaved all my hair off. My long hair was a source of identity for me, both culturally and personally. It was part of my power. It had grown down to my waist, and it was gone in seconds on that first day. Of course, I knew my head would be shaved when I enlisted; I was just not prepared for how I would feel about it. It really bothered me. Another moment I will never forget happened during the admissions process. I entered a room with 9 other young men for a physical, and was stunned when a gruff female military doctor loudly ordered us all to face forward and drop our pants for a genital health exam. It was all standard procedure; I just wasn't expecting it to be like that. I would soon discover that almost everything in the service (especially during admissions and training) was done that way; in groups, very methodically and always with a coarse, impersonal approach. With all of us awkwardly standing there shoulder to shoulder with our pants at our ankles, she sat down in a rolling office chair and began. I was second to last in the row, and as she worked her way closer and closer to me, I began to feel the same awful things that I had felt 5 years earlier in that bathroom with Emily. The doctor was all business, and completely professional as she did my exam, but it was a deeply disturbing experience for me, as the unexpected and involuntary aspects of it triggered the lingering effects of sexual abuse I had suffered throughout my childhood. Another military reality I struggled with was the constant yelling and pervasive, nonsensical rules. Again, those things touched trip-cords in my psyche, causing me to exude nervous and inappropriate physiological responses just as the genital examination had. Yet, despite negatives like those, a couple great things did happen during my time in basic training. I got into a couple fights with guys who tried to bully me and I gave them both a sound whooping. Yes, that was a good thing for a young man who had been victimized by bullies and abusers nearly his entire life. I had 19 years of pent up rage inside, and I just wasn't going to take it anymore. I also gained about 30 pounds! They *make* you eat in basic training. I had started pumping iron as well, so the two resulted in a thicker, stronger me! I'll never forget the night I laid in bed with my hands folded across my upper body, noticing that I couldn't feel my boney ribs like I used to. I had been so malnourished and severely underweight throughout my childhood, and awful kids had made fun of me because of it, calling me 'skinny', 'boney', 'stick-man', and other hurtful names. Thus, I was very happy to finally be gaining some weight. So there were some positive things about my time in the service. And yet, the reality is that I was round, and the military was square. It just wasn't a fit. And so when the arches in my feet collapsed during a training exercise one day, I was given the option to stay or go. I took the latter, and was happy to be honorably discharged. But I had done some healing there. I had fought back. I had become aware of some of my deep internal wounds. I started to find myself. I began to know who I really was. During basic training I got up to go the bathroom one night, headed out of the barracks and outside to the latrine, which was in a separate building. On my way back to bed I stopped and looked up at the starry sky. The quiet enveloped me as my contemplative consciousness opened up for the first time since I had been a small boy. I thought of all those young guys sleeping in the barracks, and sensed their life energy like a wave in my spirit. I hadn't had these kinds of feelings for so long, it felt like waking up from an induced coma. I breathed deep, taking it all in. As I gazed upward I spotted the big bear constellation (also known as the big dipper). I hadn't said a prayer since that time on the back porch when I was 11. But I said one that night as I cast my eyes on the big bear, simply asking Wakantanka to show me the way. It was a humble, small prayer. And yet, that little prayer was the beginning of a new life for me. I couldn't know it standing outside the barracks that night at 19 years of age, with a shaved head and so much damage still inside, but that constellation would shine down on me through decades of a lifetime of purpose, in times of great sorrow, and in moments of incredible triumph. And yet, the pathway back to my true self would require many years of emotional, mental, physical and sexual healing. As I left the military behind and stepped forward into the unknown, I could not have imagined how deep and how far I would have to go to mend all that was broken.

One afternoon, while I was still living in that house, I got in the car to head for my job at the department store, which was about 15 miles away. I was flat broke and so low on gas that I didn't know if I would make it to work before I ran out. I looked up and saw my dad hurriedly heading across the yard toward me as I was about to turn the key in my ignition. He came to my window and handed me a $20 bill, telling me he thought I might need it. I couldn't believe it. I was so relieved that I wouldn't end up stranded and late for work. That twenty dollars meant more to me than gas in my car. It meant my father wanted to help his son. I was so appreciative of his act of giving that day. Granted, compared to how much some parents help their kids – and how much my dad *could have* helped his – a twenty dollar bill is nothing. But in my world at that time, it was *everything*. I put $12 in the tank of my Chevelle, and kept $8 for snacks. That was my life after high school. There was no one to guide me; no one to help me. I was on my own. That $20 was it. That's all the help I ever got from either of my parents in the ensuing years after graduation. I wanted desperately to move out of that house. But I'd never had anyone teach me about money, so I was terrible with it. I couldn't save a dollar to save my life. And anyway, I didn't make enough money to pay rent even if I could find a place. Then I heard about a broken-down farmhouse about 25 miles away that had a bathroom I could live in for free, and that's where I went. I packed my things into my car and I was gone. A decade of hell faded away in my rear-view mirror, and a decade of purging lie ahead. I tore the non-working toilet out of that bathroom. Then I found a roll of old carpet some rich people had left by the road in their trash. It was covered in snow, but I dragged it onto the top of my car, held it in place with my arm and drove the 15 miles or so back to the house. My hand and arm were nearly frostbitten by the time I pulled into that country driveway. I waited a few days for it to dry and then, with only a utility knife, I cut it and laid it into place, using a hammer and nails to secure it. The plaster on the ceiling and walls was nearly all gone. I ended up finding some cheap faux-wooden paneling and put that up on the walls. The ceiling would have to stay as it was. I set up my bed, which barely fit, and that was it – *I had my own place*. Neither my dad nor my mom ever came to visit me there. And I am 99% certain that they didn't even know where it was. Years later, my wife and I gave a little reception at our home for my baby sister's achievement of an Associate's Degree from a local college. She was the only one of us four kids to earn a college degree of any kind at that time, so we wanted to celebrate it and honor her. My dad and Emily attended the party. Emily had brought a brown grocery sack with some strange items in it, the strangest being the envelope, paper-clipped to the side of it. On that envelope she had written the words *"you still owe your dad $20"*. That's right, nearly 10 years after my dad had slipped a 20 dollar bill to his son, Emily, the tyrant who had taken everything from me, *wanted it back*. I cannot overstate the flabbergasted disbelief I felt. I am proud to say, I never gave her the money. I was not the same tormented, wounded animal I had been, because during my tenure in the bathroom of that forgotten, dilapidated farmhouse in the middle of nowhere; *I had found myself*. A ton of healing would happen there. Love would find me there. I had placed a bumper sticker on the wall over my window in that bathroom that read: *God Has Given Me Prosperity*. No one could know how true that was. The greatest wealth is the freedom to be yourself, the freedom to be happy, to laugh and to hope.

And I had those things – finally. Yes indeed, God had given me what I had asked for, for so long – a place without hate, without fear and without abuse. It would be a long and winding journey back to truth, health and wellness. But I had taken the first daring step forward into the healing, and the *knowing*.

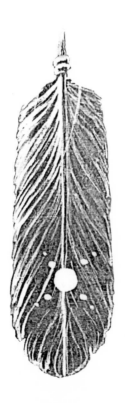

Nashoba
~ Teachers' Wisdom ~

Nashoba is a Choctaw word for wolf. It is also the given name of my dear friend and Native brother, Van. His incredible guitar work is featured on this song on the *Hidden Medicine* album, so titling it *Nashoba* just made sense. In Lakota culture, the wolf is seen as a teacher, and often shows itself to us when we need direction. In this life there are beings that come along at just the right time to teach us something, to point the way, or guide us toward our life path. They also enter our lives to help us heal and find ourselves. Teachers come in many forms. The onus is on us to learn from them when we have the chance.

My maternal grandfather died when I was 18. He was only 59 years old. Sadly, I had let about 2 years of opportunities to spend time with him slip away. Once I turned 16 I didn't need to ride my bike everywhere anymore because I had friends with cars, and we were interested in girls and just driving around listening to music. The result was I visited my grandfather less. From age 9 to 15, I had made a pretty regular thing of riding my bike over to his house at least 2 or 3 times a month. It was during some of those visits that he would tell the stories of our Lakota lineage. I credit my grandfather for instilling the Oglala Lakota identity in me. He was the one who told me "you are not white, Johnny, you are Indian with white blood". Those afternoon visits were a lifeline for me – a momentary reprieve from the abuse that seemed to corner me at every turn. At grandpa's house I was safe. And he imparted a lot of wisdom over the years. Through the lens of the Lakota familial experience my grandpa gave me, I was able to consider another view of oppression besides the very personal version I endured at home. That broader scope was a gift that helped me to gain a perspective outside myself. Through those true stories of Lakota struggle, I gained an understanding that the hurt being inflicted on me was merely a perpetuation of generations of suffering my ancestors had been subjected to. In short, I was not alone. The alcoholism, drug abuse and deep dysfunction I saw in my family had a root – a reason. Those destructive behaviors were born of great, unimaginable loss that went back centuries. And that loss was manifesting in the quiet despair of substance abuse and unhealthy choices. I know because I have seen it – historical trauma lives on in the genes. That knowledge helped me to see beyond my own pain, and planted a seed that would one day grow to be my complete identity as a man.

Donny had met a girl. Her name was Amy, and she wanted him to go to church with her. Neither Donny nor I were the churchy type, but he was into that gal so he begged me to come along with him. Though I had been forced to go to Sunday school a few times as a boy, I had always hated it. When they would make us sing '*It's a Happy Day*', it seemed so artificial. It felt like a lie. My spirituality had always been experienced in the woods, far outside the doors of organized religion. Thus, I had zero interest in getting up early to go to some church, but Donny was my bud, so I agreed to go. During the service, I noticed a guy sitting about 4 rows in front of us who had long hair like me, and was sporting a heavy metal shirt of some kind. I wondered what he was doing there, and figured he was probably in a similar situation to mine, having been dragged to church by a friend or some girl. Donny and I were terrible that morning. The pastor had big, buggy eyes and was kind of a goofy looking dude, and we could barely conceal our hysteria. Donny tried to behave for Amy's sake, but every time he looked at me, we would both lose it and have to fight back the laughter. Finally, the service ended, at which point the pastor gestured to the guy with the long hair and asked him, "Mark, would you close us in prayer?" I couldn't believe it. *That* guy was going to pray?! Did I see that right? As everyone bowed their heads, I kept one eye on him. Sure enough, it was he who spoke. And as he uttered the first words of his prayer, I had a feeling come over me I hadn't experienced since I had been a 5-year-old boy talking to Spirit in the woods. This guy prayed like God was in the room, and it moved me deep inside. Afterward, as Donny, Amy and I all made our way out of the church; I couldn't take my eyes off Mark. That long-haired, heavy metal dude *knew* God, and I wanted to know more. So, for the first time in my life, I started going to church. I got to know Mark, and I can tell you, his spiritual life was the real deal. He was also the lead singer of a Christian rock band, and had a fantastic voice. Not only that, Mark was a genuinely great guy and I liked him a lot. In fact, I admired him and even looked up to him. I had never thought much of Christianity, but now I was learning more about it than I had ever fathomed possible. I got very involved, even becoming the front man for several Christian Metal bands myself. I studied The Bible front to back, even exploring the Greek and Hebrew texts, using a concordance. I was in deep. That buggy-eyed pastor ended up getting caught in a scandal, and Mark stepped in to lead the church. Not long after that, he asked me to be his assistant pastor, and I accepted. Things went okay for a while, but I began to slip into religious fundamentalism and ended up in a bad place spiritually. I had become a judgmental zealot, and I was a stranger to myself. You see, fundamentalism and abuse require the same ingredient – *fear*. So there was a psychologically unhealthy and potentially self-destructive familiarity that caused me to fall prey to it. It was at that time that the seeds of Lakota knowledge planted in me by my grandfather years earlier saved me from myself. I walked away from the church, and back into the woods. Spiritual wisdom awaited me there in the quiet places I had known from my youth, and it helped me to sort out the myriad of questions I had. With time and contemplation, answers came, and I made peace with Wakantanka/God, and found truth, balance and love in my personal walk with Spirit. I turned away from judgment and embraced humility. I traded condemnation for grace. I have Mark to thank for that. His prayer at the conclusion of the church service that morning opened up my soul, and ultimately played an important part in bringing me to where I am today spiritually. What a gift he gave me. What a gift.

As I have shared already, my high school years left little to be desired. And yet, during that time there were two men who made an indelible mark on my life: George and Don. For all the shortcomings of a small town country high school, there was one shining exception; they had an actual radio station on site. George approached me one day and said he thought I had a great speaking voice, and should consider taking his radio broadcasting class. The idea of talking on a microphone with classmates listening on the other end was more than a little unnerving, but it sounded interesting, so I signed up. My time in that class is part of the reason I am sitting here writing this book, and why there is an album that goes with it, and why I have performed and spoken all over the world. Quite literally, I found my voice in that radio broadcasting class. It was a perfect scenario to draw an emotionally abused introvert out of hiding because, although I was required to speak to an audience on a microphone, I was actually alone in that broadcasting booth. Spirit could not have concocted a more ingenious way to help me begin to restore my self-confidence. I got an A in that class, and even went on to work in radio for a bit after high school. George could never know just how desperately I needed it, but his belief in me at that tumultuous time in my life was a buoy that helped keep me from drowning. It was a gentle, guiding nudge that altered the trajectory of my life. Don was another encourager. He was the one who convinced me to audition for a role in the Jr. Play. Most of the 11th grade students who tried out for the play were the popular kids in school, and that fact alone made me a nervous wreck, which adversely affected my audition. The result being that I was given a tiny bit part with one appearance and one line in the whole play. That fact sure made rehearsals a breeze! A popular athletic kid named Steve had gotten the lead. It was about half way into the several month rehearsal schedule when Don called me during my after-school radio program one afternoon. He informed me that he had kicked Steve out of the play, and wanted to know if I would consider taking the lead role. I said yes. I went home that night and asked my siblings for help. My 'late arrival' as the lead had me starting over a month behind the rest of the cast, and I wanted to prove something to all those popular kids. Over the weekend I completely immersed myself in memorizing the play, my brother and sisters all reading the script with me again and again and again. I recited my lines until I was totally sick of it, and then I did it some more. Thus, when I arrived for my first rehearsal in the lead role, I performed the entire first act *off book*! The cast was amazed, and so was Don. I was so proud of myself for pulling that off. The play was a comedy, and after nearly choking and forgetting my first line on opening night, I was off with a bang. I found out I had a knack for theater performance, and that I could make people laugh; a huge boost for my self-esteem. There was one small discomfort. The very pretty, popular girl named Deb, who had gotten the role of the wife of the lead character, could barely conceal her disdain at having to play that role with me. Regardless, I came away from that experience feeling better about myself than I had in years. Don asked me back for the senior play the next year and I got the lead in that show too. He believed in me, and because he did, I began to believe too. Like George, Don had reached out to me, and his trust in my abilities had made a lasting effect on the path my life would take. Both of these men taught me to value myself, and their lessons live on every time I take a stage.

There have been so many teachers along the way. In Lakota culture, there is a character in our childhood stories we call *Iktomi*. *Iktomi* literally means spider, but the character is more of a heyoka (sacred clown) or trickster who, by his bad behavior, teaches us how *not* to live. In some ways I see *Iktomi* in my mother and father. Often, they taught me by their bad choices; but not always. I learned a lot of good things from my mom and dad too. They were kind and decent people. One time a guy had stolen $20 from my dad and he knew it. When I asked why he wouldn't confront the thief, my dad replied "because twenty dollars is a small price to pay to own a man's conscience". Those words taught me that money is not more important than honor. So my dad was certainly a teacher. And the hawks have always circled over my life, imparting visions when I needed them. I have learned valuable lessons from my siblings and my friends. And the Elders who graced my path have all guided me with their wisdom. One such Elder is my Muscogee Creek friend Twofeathers. With gentle humor and a twinkle in his eye, he has taught me many truths and explained many mysteries. He is one of the wisest men I have ever known. Never pretentious and always self-effacing, he has shown me a great deal about how to walk with Spirit in this life and remain grounded and real. It was Twofeathers who was there with me and a few others on that day in the sacred place shortly after my mother had died, which I wrote about in the prologue. Earlier that afternoon, I had felt her spiritual essence come over me as I had sat in stillness in a special place. I had kept that moment to myself. Later on, as I quietly walked past that area with Twofeathers, he turned to me and simply said "your mother is back there". I was surprised, and replied "yes, she is", and he gently squeezed my shoulder. Nothing more was said. Moments like that are why I love him, and have such an appreciation for his gift. He is truly a great teacher, and I am blessed to call him my friend. And so the lessons, and those who share them, come in many ways, and it is up to us to absorb their wisdom and hidden medicine. For those teachers are like the wolf, who appears in the cavern after a great flood, and leads us out of the darkness.

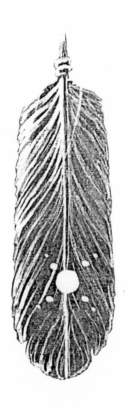

Surrender
~ Letting Go of Hurt ~

We human beings could learn a lot from watching the snake. Every so often during its life, the snake does something wonderful that we often fail to do – it sheds its skin. That transformative renewal gives the snake a fresh start. There are moments throughout our life that afford us a chance to begin anew, an opportunity to shed an old skin, and heal a festering wound. And there is a secret to completing that process that we can also learn by observing what the snake does – *it leaves its old skin behind*. We, on the other hand, have a tendency to hold onto the skins we shed, dragging them around like baggage. And over time, the oppressive weight of all those unhealthy things we hold onto can crush our chances for complete healing, and cripple our ability to reach our full potential. But shedding our damaged skin is not easy. We must first face the wounds that haven't healed, and address them. That can be a painful undertaking, but we have to do it if we are to take the next steps toward wellness. Once our wounds are closed and only the scars remain, it is time to pour out the pain, which can be difficult as well. Sometimes we can hurt others when we vent in inappropriate ways, but healing is a messy business. It is rarely easy. Letting go of hurt begins by first acknowledging it. After that, we need to express our feelings about it. This is where a counselor, trusted friend or loved one can help. We just need someone to listen, to hear us. And this is not a one-time thing; it can take years of crying, raging and sharing to exercise all the demons of our suffering. But once we have, there comes a moment when we have to make a conscious choice – do we hold on to the hurt or release it? What we decide will mean the difference between a life of misery and a life of joy. Thus, in order to fully heal, we must let go. We *must* let go.

Sometimes the damaging effects of child abuse result in physical maladies, and addressing those afflictions can require everything from psychological counseling to a medical procedure, depending on the severity of the issue. For me, it required surgery. You may recall me mentioning in *The Long Walk* chapter, that a urinary tract infection – which put an end to the bed-wetting in my mid-teens – would persist for eight more years, and that I would divulge why later. This is a sensitive area, but to omit this part of my story would be a disservice to anyone who has suffered abuse and needs to know they are not alone as they face the enormity of the healing process. So I will again be honest, but gentle. It was during my time living in the bathroom of that farmhouse that the burning during urination came roaring back. I was about 21 years old, and had been dealing with a constant urinary tract infection since I was 15. Back then, it had been so bad that my dad took me to see a doctor. I was thoroughly examined and it was determined that everything was in working order, so I was given some pills to take. The medicine seemed to help, and the infection subsided. But the burning always returned. It came and went like that for years. Until that morning at the farmhouse, when I woke up with the urge and discovered that I couldn't urinate at all. I panicked. I had no insurance, no money and I was nowhere near a hospital. But I knew I was in trouble, so I quickly got dressed and headed out the door. I drove like a madman to the closest hospital, which was easily an hour away, and went to the emergency room. The need to empty my bladder had become almost intolerable by the time they got me in. The doctor attempted to catheterize me – which, by the way, was the most physically painful experience of my life – but was unsuccessful. However the effort broke something free, and I was finally able to urinate, albeit very painfully. Unable to afford a stay in the hospital, much less pay for an emergency room procedure, I opted to go back home. There would be a few more of those panicked hospital visits and brutal, failed catheterization attempts over the coming two years. I had another complete blockage occur during my best friend Kelly's wedding. I was a groomsman, and was able to make it through the marriage ceremony, but I never made the reception, as I slipped away and rushed to the hospital. I never said a thing to Kelly that day, as I did not want to put a damper on his big moment. Ultimately, things could not go on like that much longer, and I would be forced to face the infirmity in my body once and for all, and finally heal the dysfunction that caused it.

And so it was that, at 23 years of age, and after suffering for eight long years with a severe, ongoing urinary tract infection, I ended up finally having surgery. Well, make that *two* surgeries. The first procedure was unsuccessful, and I woke up in post op with a tube coming out of my pelvis. As it turned out, the damage to my urethra was so bad it would take one more surgical procedure to finish the job. After that second urinary tract surgery, I awoke to the realization that I was catheterized, and learned that I would have to remain in that condition for almost two weeks until everything healed inside. That was the longest two weeks of my life. I went back to my bathroom/bedroom in that country farmhouse and passed the days in extreme and constant discomfort. Any sort of bodily movement was difficult, and the daily occurrence of nocturnal penile tumescence caused by the catheter made mornings nearly intolerable. I was helpless. A female friend I had met through the Christian music world offered to come out and give me a hand during that period. I resisted, as my condition was obviously quite awkward, but she showed up anyway. And nearly every day for two weeks she did my laundry, brought me food, and basically ensured that I could remain stationary as much as possible. To accept her help, I had to relinquish my need for control. I had to let go, and surrender. She took charge, and made sure I had what I needed. I'd never had anyone care enough to help me like that. It was a first. And a seed was planted that, years later, would bloom into something beautiful. Finally, the day came for me to go to the doctor and have the catheter removed. A buddy named Ron who had multiple sclerosis offered to drive my car, which at that time was a rusted out 77' Monte Carlo. We headed out, running late as usual. The ride was brutal, as it seemed even the smallest bump made that old car shudder and shake. We weren't halfway there when we got a flat tire on the highway. I couldn't believe it. As usual, I had no spare, so we were stranded. We had already been running late, now I would likely miss my appointment. I was beside myself. After years of suffering, months of surgery, and two weeks of struggling to even walk, all I wanted was to get that damn tube out of my penis. Now, it didn't look like that was going to happen. Ron, whose condition had considerably affected his gate over the years, began hobbling down the roadside trying to thumb a ride. We were something to see! In hindsight, it was downright hysterical. Ron, with his long, scraggly hair, heavy metal t-shirt and MS limp – and I, with my long hair, worn out rock n roll jeans, and painful, catheterized shuffle… I had zero hope that anyone would pick us up looking the way we did. But Ron hadn't held his thumb out for more than a few minutes when a shiny, brand-new black Lincoln pulled over. The man behind the wheel was a white guy who looked to be in his early 60s. He was wearing a black suit and tie, and had a full head of perfectly groomed white hair and a trimmed white beard. He asked where we were headed, and promptly offered us a ride. I was amazed. I got in the back seat and shut the door. He pulled onto the highway, and I immediately noticed the difference – that car rode like it was floating on air. I never felt a single bump. As he made small talk with us, I began to look around his car. There wasn't a spot of dirt anywhere. Not even a piece of fuzz on the floor – and I knew a thing or two about that from my childhood. There was not a hair on his shoulders, or a speck of dust on the center console. It was all a little *too* perfect. I began to wonder who this guy was. Was he even real? Were Ron and I being entertained by an angel? I'll never know, but I can tell you this: when he dropped us off at the front door of the doctor's office, we were 15 minutes early.

Finally, it was done. The catheter was removed. I was free! After that, the doctor asked me to take a seat so he could have a chat with me. There was one more thing he had to fix. He proceeded to tell me that my urinary tract infection had been one of the worst he had ever seen in his 25-year career. He followed that comment with an explanation of where the infection had been in my body, using a medical illustration of the male anatomy to help me understand. The location of the damage had been deep inside, right where the ejaculatory duct merges with the urethra. A fact which the doctor proposed could have been caused by a regular habit of intentionally holding back seminal emission during sexual release. He asked if that was the case with me, and I replied that it was, adding that I hadn't known any other way since I was 13-years-old. After hearing that, he explained that it was something I should cease doing, as it was why I ended up needing surgery. Thus, for reasons which were deeply rooted in the abuse I had suffered as a child – I had developed a very unhealthy sexual dysfunction that had ultimately inflicted severe physical damage to the most sensitive parts of my body, resulting in one of the worst cases of male urinary tract infection my veteran doctor had ever seen. So it is, that the wounds live on long after the abuse stops, manifesting in ways we may not expect. But it is up to us to address those festering injuries, no matter how difficult, if we are to ever become whole again. Healing is hard. I know this, and yet I have always found it ironic, that sometimes we must hurt, to heal the pain.

I woke up late that night with a familiar urge I hadn't felt in weeks! I hustled downstairs in the dark and out the back door. A full moon was shining down as I stood there. At first I was afraid to go. It had been so long since I had peed without pain. So I waited for a few minutes. Finally, I found my courage, and for the first time in over a month, urinated like a regular guy.

There was no pain! I breathed a deep sigh of relief, and began to cry. 8 years…. That was how long it had been since it hadn't hurt to pee. Abuse can open a wound and steal away even something as basic as a normal bodily function. It can break us in ways that take decades to mend. At long last, I had faced my affliction. Thankfully, that doctor had fixed what had been broken for so long, and permanently healed my urinary tract and sexual dysfunction. But a deeper healing took place in my soul, as I pulled that abusive weed out at the root and released it into the ether. Like the snake, I had shed an old skin and let it go.

There was still so much healing to do. So much hurt to face, pain to address and dysfunction to release. I remember talking with my brother one day and hearing him tell me how long it had taken him to open the refrigerator in his own house without feeling nervous about it. He was not alone; I too, had struggled with that. The years of food abuse – yes, that's what I call it – had taken their toll. Food became a chronic control issue. Having been nearly starved during my teens, my body had developed a kind of physiological 'off' switch for my appetite which would engage after I had only eaten enough to barely feed a bird. Thus, my want for food would shut off well before my need for nourishment was reached. In short, my stomach felt stuffed, but it was actually not full. I had developed that survival mechanism to stave off the hunger pangs I experienced when I was forbidden to eat during my years as a growing teenage boy. And that malfunction – which has stayed with me to this day – made achieving a healthy weight a monumental effort. When I graduated from high school, I was 6 foot 3 inches tall, and weighed only 125 pounds. These days, when well-meaning people tell me how 'lucky' I am for not being able to gain weight, they could not imagine how untrue that is. And when folks unwittingly call me 'skinny', they could never fathom the pain that word has caused me, nor how hard I have worked in the weight room to avoid hearing it. One day, while visiting with my dear friend Morten from Norway, who is also a survivor of child abuse, I shared something that took my wife by surprise. Peggy knew more details about the effects of my abusive childhood than anyone, and yet even she was taken aback as I confessed how an irrational fear would come over me sometimes when I was in the shower and she hollered for me. That holler from my loving wife would trigger an emotional response that was not tied to the present, but rooted in the trauma of the past. Nobody was more sensitive to my issues than Peggy, and yet she was unaware of that one. Over the years, my wife has been my champion, counselor, healer and biggest supporter. No one has believed in me more than her. And yet, the journey an abuse survivor takes to heal is a lonely one. I think Peggy would agree. Still, she has helped me to see so much.

I want to tell you about the tiger and the mouse. I had a favorite stuffed animal as a boy. It was a tiger. I clung to it at night when I was afraid and confused. It was my comforter. During the move to dad and Emily's house it was lost, and I was heartbroken. It was never replaced – until decades later, when Peggy surprised me with a brand new one. I now keep my new tiger by my bed as a symbol of love and healing. Then there was the mouse. My siblings and I all had a handful of stuffed animals; teddy bears, dinosaurs and such. Out of the blue one day, Emily came to our rooms with a garbage bag and made us put them all in it so they could go out with the trash. We were all very sad as we gathered our fuzzy friends and watched them get tossed. I remember walking past the trash bags by the street the next morning on the way to school and thinking about my stuffed animals inside them. When I came home they were gone. A short time later I was searching my room for something and discovered that one of my stuffed animals had avoided detection – a small, pink mouse. That little stuffed mouse was like me; it had survived by staying hidden. I slept with that mouse for years, and always kept him a secret. I still have him today. He sits on my dresser, and every now and then I pick him up, give him a squeeze, and reflect on how far we have come together. The tiger and the mouse; in so many ways I am like them both.

Mother's Day was coming, and I was, as usual, planning to send *two* cards – one to Mumma and yes, one to Emily. Peggy stopped me in my tracks when she asked me why I would do that. My only response was that I didn't know; I had just always done it. Her question forced me to seriously consider why I would send a Mother's Day card to a woman who had so badly abused me. Why would I do that? After some self-examination, I determined that the real reason I had always sent a Mother's Day card to Emily was *fear*. I was *still* afraid of her. Even as a grown man she terrified me, and I didn't want to risk incurring her wrath. Abuse does a curious thing to its victims. It manipulates and warps the lens by which we process stimuli, causing us to misinterpret it and respond inappropriately. This is why victims of abuse can suffer such extreme social disorders, because we are viewing the world through a looking glass in which things are either inaccurately magnified or are actually 'closer than they appear'. Neither perception can be trusted. It can be huge when someone helps us to see things more clearly, but it is up to us to listen, *and to act*. I never sent another card to Emily. That first year was scary, as I nervously passed the days fully expecting the worst. But nothing ever happened. Funny how you can be so afraid, and discover how little there was to fear. So, although the release of old dead skin does help lighten the load, the remnants of abuse remain. Even after all the healing I have done. Some things will be with me to the end. That is the reality. We who have suffered at the hands of another know this truth. And that profound acceptance is by far the most powerful facet of the act of *surrender*.

Firebird

~ Rising From The Ashes ~

There is an ancient indigenous legend about a man who was taken by his enemies, dragged to a clearing and thrown into a great fire. The men laughed as he was consumed by the flames, celebrating their terrible deed. Then, something in the glowing embers shifted and turned. There, in the belly of the raging fire, they saw it, and watched in silent horror as a being began to appear. Before their terrified eyes, it swelled, lifted and rose from the ashes, spreading its wings of flame. Where, before, there had been a mere man, now stood the *Firebird*. And his enemies were never seen or heard from again. I have faced a lot. I dug deep to drag myself out of the ditch child abuse threw me into. Before that ditch, I was a beautiful happy boy, full of innocent wonder and hopeful promise. I crawled out the other side a ragged, wounded and broken young man. The fires of hate had consumed me, but I had survived. The journey back would be long and torturous. The rising would be painful, and would require a ton of courage and a lot of help. I would have to accept what I had lost, and reclaim what I could save. I would have to take the shattered remnants of myself and painstakingly piece together a new vision of who I was. I had been burned down to nothing, but there was still life in the embers.

It was between the ages of 19 and 25 that I began the journey back to my indigenous center. Reflections from my early childhood bubbled back to the surface, and I began to remember who I had always been. The two visions I had as a boy started to crystallize and make sense. I had gleaned enough from my grandfather, parents and others during my formative years to have a sense of identity. As I shared in a previous chapter, it is not easy being a Native person of mixed ancestry. Sometimes people ridicule those who try to assert their Native identity. My dad rarely mentioned anything about his Indian blood. However, on one occasion he told his friends that he was Potawatomi, and they laughed at him, telling him he surely must be making it up because they had never heard of such a tribe. To prove himself, my father went to a Potawatomi casino and bought himself a ball cap with the tribal name on it and showed it to them. Point being, when a person of mixed ancestry identifies with the American Indian part of their lineage, it can be met with skepticism and insults. In my memory bag, there is a paper I wrote in 3rd grade in which I tell how it felt to be Indian in a world that didn't see you or accept you. So, you see, the matter of identity was settled in me long ago. And once I finally escaped the tyranny of abuse, my hunger to learn more began to return. The Lakota wisdom imparted in my youth began to whisper to the yearning I had within. I found solace in old prayers, old songs and old ways. Despite everything; I had beaten the odds. The flames of abuse had burned me down, but I was rising. I was rising.

After a couple years of friendship, and a few more years of dating, I married Peggy. I was 26, and it was the happiest day of my life. The marriage also made me a step-father to 3 children. A few years later we adopted a daughter through the Indian Child Welfare program. A lifetime of horrible step-parent experiences had soured me on the whole 'step' thing. So, from day one, I was just 'John', and I strove to give them all the love I never got from the 'steps' in my life. Shortly after our wedding, Peggy's sister Suzie had helped me get work at a box factory. During the 7 years prior to that I had gone through more jobs than most people would in two lifetimes. I had been in the military, worked on the back of a garbage truck, in a department store, at a fast-food restaurant, a radio station, as a tractor-trailer driver, a construction worker, and farm laborer. I had tried selling vacuum cleaners, drove a large newspaper delivery route, and finally, worked at more factories than I care to remember. I rarely lasted more than a few months in any of those jobs. I was not content. I wanted more out of my life. I had watched my father's hopes waste away during decades in a factory, and didn't want that to happen to me. All my life, I had dreamed of music. It was the music I first heard in the phonograph when I was 4-

years-old that had awakened my soul. And it was music I escaped to during the hellish years of abuse. Music had saved me then, and I needed it to save me again. I had tried. I fronted two very talented, popular rock bands and then performed folk music as a solo singer-songwriter act. But nothing ever panned out, and I needed money to live. So, I would resign myself to taking some job I didn't want and endure the drudgery of it for a while. I was *always* late to work. A fact that got me fired from a lot of places. My whole life I had been on 'Indian time', and have always been the last one out the door. But my showing up late for work wasn't because of that, I just didn't care enough about what I was doing to be on time. If I didn't get fired, the misery would overwhelm me and I would quit. So, although I appreciated that Suzie had pulled some strings for me, I was not entirely thrilled about taking yet another job in a factory. I could feel my dreams starting to slip away, and the thought of ending up in a life of quiet desperation and unfulfilled promise like my father terrified me and kept me awake at night. But my wife knew me. She had fallen in love with a music man who had big aspirations, and who she realized would never be content to toil away in a meaningless endeavor his entire life. Peggy was also privy to having heard nearly everything there was to hear about my abusive childhood, and she had become my strongest advocate. So, when she called me one day and asked me to meet her at a Chinese restaurant after work to discuss an idea she had, my heart leapt with hopeful anticipation. I couldn't wait for my shift to end that day. As I drove to meet her I wondered what could possibly be so important that she felt the need to talk about it over a meal. The suspense was nearly killing me by the time I sat down with her at the restaurant. With a twinkle in her big brown eyes, she began. I had been thinking about buying a snowmobile, and had my eye on one. Peggy knew that, and offered me a proposition: we could take the money we had saved and buy the snowmobile, or we could put that money toward opening a Native American retail store – and I could quit my job. The decision was all mine to make. Either option was fine with her, but the choice was up to me. I didn't hesitate. My response was immediate. Yes, yes, yes. I had quit so many jobs, what would one more matter? I had survived so much. Taking a financial risk was small potatoes by comparison. I had done that one many times before, and was not at all afraid of it. I didn't know it then, but that meeting was an answer to a prayer. The music was whispering, holding out its hand and reaching for me through the ether, and my life would never be the same. That pivotal moment changed everything. It was the beginning of all that was to come. After so many failures and heartbreaking disappointments, it was that little meeting where I chose a dream over a snowmobile which would ultimately result in my eventual success as a musician. I am so grateful to Peggy for her courage and her faith.

She has always believed. Oh, by the way, the name of the Chinese restaurant where we made that life-changing decision: *The Fortune House*. A more fitting title for the start of a new life I cannot conceive.

We called it *'Red Earth'*, and got busy making contacts with Native artisans, suppliers and wholesalers. We stocked our store with everything from world-class American Indian wall art, to sculptures, silver jewelry, handmade traditional items and more. We also sold Native books, music cassettes and even art pieces my brother and I created. After a lot of work, we finally opened our doors for business. It was an exciting moment for me. I had never done anything like that, and it made me very proud. I loved that little store. It was around that time I got involved in live theater again. Peggy had noticed an audition announcement in the paper for a show, and encouraged me to give it a shot. I went for it, and got a nice part. The play was a success, and immediately following its wrap, I was approached by a director who made it clear he wanted me to audition for the lead role in his upcoming production – the Broadway musical version of *The Will Rogers Follies*. I was hooked, so I gave it a whirl, and for the 3rd time in my life, got the lead role. It was a massive show, and I was the star! Playing Will Rogers was one of the great honors of my life. He was a Cherokee renaissance man, a rope-spinning cowboy comedian, actor, philosopher and writer who became the voice of hope for many Americans during The Great

Depression. The role was huge, and entailed learning thousands of lines, dozens of songs and dances, and – as if all that weren't enough – I had to learn to perform rope tricks! I watched and listened to hours of footage and tape of Will. I wanted to do more than 'portray' him, I wanted to *channel* him. In the end, the enormous production was a smashing success, as we sold out every night and received rave reviews. Shortly after the show wrapped I was tending shop at *'Red Earth'*, when a woman named Dorothy came in who had attended one of the *Follies* performances and saw our ad in the program. She proceeded to inform me that she worked with an educational living history group who needed an American Indian presenter, and wanted to know if I would be interested in filling that position. After observing their very top-notch outdoor setup, I signed on, and began presenting the Native American portion of their program shortly thereafter. A few months later, I was attending a powwow. As I took in the sound of drum and voice, I perused the vendors, looking for possibilities for our store. It was during that little stroll that I came upon a booth that was selling Native flutes for kids. I decided a flute would be an interesting addition to my living history program, and they were cheap, so I bought one. I could not have fathomed in my wildest imagination where that humble little flute was going to take me. I brought it to my next outing and played it for the 4th graders. Their reactions amazed me. They folded their hands and closed their eyes in prayer;

they assumed meditation-type poses; they imitated my movements, and mimed my playing. It was beautiful to watch. Over the next several years I was gifted a few nicer flutes as I continued my work with the living history program. I also began to give cultural talks at universities; always using the flutes as merely a small part of those presentations. And all this I did while we continued to run our shop. After about 3 years, a large Native American retail chain with way more money opened right around the corner from us, and dealt a fatal blow to our business. Our little store struggled, and finally closed. It was a sad thing to turn out the lights and lock that door for the last time. What exacerbated my heartache was that, because 'Red Earth' failed, I was about to start work at another factory. This time it was General Motors, the so-called 'holy grail' of all the assembly line jobs you could get in Michigan. But there was nothing about it that seemed 'holy' to me. Once again, I felt like my dreams were dying. What I couldn't see through my downcast, watery eyes was that a seed had been planted. 'Red Earth' was in the ground, but not dead. It had been consumed by the flames of our enemies, but it would one day rise again, transformed into something new. And I too, would remake myself in my own image, rise from the ashes, and become what I was always destined to be.... the *Firebird*.

Claiming Breath
~ Honor Thyself ~

To fully heal from abuse, we must cast into the sea the former things and begin anew. No longer can we accept as absolute truth the self-image that was shaped by the horrors of our past. Neither can we allow others to tell us who they think we should be. On the contrary; it is up to us to decide who we are, and to pick up our broken pieces, add new ones, and rebuild our personhood. This challenging process is one of the final steps in the circular healing journey we take from joy to despair and back. And it requires enormous courage. We must be willing to assert our right to be who we choose to be. That can mean losing relationships with people we thought were our friends and sometimes, even family members. Monumental change is necessary if we are to ever completely break free from the chains of negative self-perception that bind us and keep us from rising up and realizing a new vision for our life. Our breath is ours, it belongs to us and us alone, and we must lay claim to it once and for all.

My days at General Motors began, and I settled in to life on the assembly line – again. My dad was the one who had put my name into the pool for prospective new-hires, and when I got the job it made him feel good that he had been able to do something for me. I, on the other hand, did not feel so good about having to go to work there. After *'Red Earth'* closed, Peggy and I nursed our wounds, picked up the pieces and got busy formulating a 3-year plan: we would save our money and ultimately sell everything, quit our jobs and move 1,000 miles away to the ancient Ozark Mountains of northwest Arkansas to launch a full-time music career. To anyone else, that idea might have seemed reckless and ill-fated. In fact, I heard through the grapevine that at least one member of my extended family had said I was a fool for quitting my job at General Motors, and that I would never make the money at music I had made at that factory. Well, we were going to see about that. In the meantime, there was a new thing called 'the internet' that you could access on a computer. I had also heard that businesses were going onto the 'world wide web' and setting up 'websites' to sell their wares. We had a computer that had been given to us by a lifelong member of Peggy's family, a catholic priest named Father Bob who, by the way, had officiated our wedding. I had learned programming in high school, long before there were user interfaces like Windows, but I didn't even know how to turn this computer on! However, like almost everything I had ever done in my life, I figured it out on my own. A web-designer named Scott was recommended to us by a friend, and we hired him to build our first website: NativeCircle.com. When he started, I explained to him that this was a Native American site and therefore I would want it to be designed in a way that reflected that. He assured me that he 'got it', and would send me some pages to look at soon. A week or so later, we got to see what he had built, and I wasn't thrilled. He hadn't 'gotten it' after all, and Peggy called to go over some of the changes I wanted him to make. He responded by saying that I should "stick to making dream catchers and leave the web-design to him". Yep, he actually said that. Needless to say, we fired him, and again, I had to figure it out on my own. With the help of a great guy at our web-hosting company, I took the reins and built the first incarnation of the Native Circle website, which had an online store named – you guessed it – *'Red Earth'*! And thus, our little retail store was reborn, and it has been with us ever since. Native Circle, which has been redesigned numerous times over its long internet life, is today the longest continuously running Native American site on the web. Not long after its inception, another site came along. It would be my namesake: JohnTwoHawks.com.

Once I got acquainted with some of the folks at General Motors, I began to share with them as we passed the hours putting wheels on Chevy Cavaliers. I told them my plan was to only be there for 3 years, after which I was going to walk away and jump into my music career full time. Most of them were doubtful of that. They told me I would eventually change my mind because the pay and the benefits would be so good by then I wouldn't want to quit. But none of those great guys and gals I worked with could have fathomed the depth of my resolve. I was more determined than I had ever been. I would make it *this* time. I was going to build my strength, store up my power, and when the moment of truth came, I would run and leap with everything I had into the night and become a shooting star. The days, weeks and months dragged by and finally turned into 3 years. At last, the time had come. We had sold everything except what we needed to sell most – our home. But we were as ready as we would ever be, and could wait no longer. We put our house up for rent, packed our things and prepared to go. I will never forget my last day at General Motors. As I went around the shop shaking hands and giving hugs, I was struck by two distinct, visible reactions from my workmates. In some, I saw a genuine happiness. These contented folks were rooting for me. In others, however, I sensed a subtle sadness, almost as if they wanted to walk out that door with me. That observation moved me deeply, and I have never forgotten it. Whenever the challenges of my music career become difficult, I remember the faces of those good people who, without saying a word, spoke volumes to my soul, and I turn and hold my wings into the swirling winds and find the updraft.

And so, we did it. We moved 1,000 miles away from everything I had ever known. Nobody knew me in this place. There were no preconceived notions. No prior perceptions and no familiar spirits. I could start over. I would redefine my persona, and at long last, be who I had always been inside. A short while later, our house finally sold. That experience turned into a brief but intense nightmare. Our renters had trashed the place, and we had to go back up and clean it out for the new owners – one who turned out to be a full-blown alcoholic. It was a hellish return to that last remnant of our former life, and as we drove out of there for the last time after all that craziness, we never looked back. We took some of the maza ska (money) from the sale of our house and invested it in performance and recording equipment, as well as the replication of my first two albums on CD. We started with nothing, and bit by bit, step by step, we grew a company, and I began to make a name for myself in the music world. What began with small performances in humble places became sold out concerts in overseas arenas. It didn't happen overnight. It was a long, long road that pushed the limits of all my abilities and tested my resolve time and time again. It demanded absolute laser-focus, an unrelenting determination and a ton of hard work. But the payoff was worth it all. Our calculated risk, which some thought was foolishness, landed me on the red carpet at Paramount Pictures, and then the Grammys, and more importantly helped me achieve the greatest accomplishment of all: self-healing. It wasn't easy, but I took a stand. I claimed my breath, and my life. No one would ever tell me who I was again, nor presume to define or confine me with false assumptions about who they, or anyone else, thought I was. I alone would speak my truth. Many years after I had left that job at General Motors, I rolled into a nearby town on a concert tour. At the 'meet and greet' after the show, I looked up from my autograph table to see a guy I had worked with at the factory back then standing there. He had come to my concert that night, and with eyes welling up, told me how proud he was of me, and that he couldn't wait to tell the gang at work the next day that ol' Two-Hawks had succeeded, and made it to the top of the mountain. It brought tears to my eyes as I got up and he gave me a strong bear-hug. He will never know how much that meant to me.

It was at another tour stop in Michigan that the strangest thing I have ever experienced after a concert occurred. At intermission, a crew member came and delivered a message to me from Peggy – *Emily* was in the audience. I couldn't get my head around it. Why? She hadn't seen or heard from me since my father's funeral 6 years earlier. So why would she come? To this day, I still don't know the answer. But I made my mind up that night; somehow, I would find a way during the second act of my show to make mention of the fact that I was a survivor of terrible child abuse. And I did. Just saying those words out loud, knowing that she was somewhere out there in the dark listening, was cathartic. But then the show ended, and the 'meet and greet' began. And I was mortified to be informed that Emily was *in the line*. Peggy, not wanting to make a scene, informed me that she was leaving and heading for the hotel room. I had mixed emotions about her decision. On the one hand I was glad, because I knew how Peggy felt about Emily, and I didn't want there to be a scene in the lobby either. And yet, on the other hand, her leaving meant it was just me, and a handful of staff who knew nothing of the monster that was approaching me in that line. But I agreed, it was best for Peggy to go. With each autograph and brief exchange, I got more and more nervous. I am normally 100% engaged with each person who comes to my autograph table after a concert, giving them my full attention. But that night, I could barely concentrate on those poor people ahead of Emily in the line. All I could think was; what on earth was I going to say to her once she got to my table? Why was she even there? An old, familiar fear rippled through my body for a fleeting moment. And then I glanced down at the personal, spiritual power symbols beaded onto the front of my sacred traditional regalia, and realized *I was untouchable*. I was wearing impenetrable armor. As she approached, I took a deep breath; expanding my chest, and straightening my spine; standing tall and intensely peering down at her from my 6 foot 3-inch frame with a stoic Lakota face fit for an Edward Curtis photo. As she looked up, cowering before me with her pale face and mousy eyes, I spoke. In a deep, emotionless voice, I simply said "Emily? What are you doing?" You could've cut the air with a knife. She timidly muttered something I cannot recall because I wasn't listening anyway. I no longer cared what she said. I wasn't afraid anymore. Seconds later she was gone from my table, and I have never seen her since.

I remember studying a map of the USA when I was a boy, looking for the place in the continental, contiguous United States that was the absolute furthest from where I lived in Michigan. I found it in Yuma, Arizona, and decided I would move there just as soon as I could get out of that God-forsaken state! I apologize to anyone who lives in Michigan and loves it. I am aware that it has its beauty, and I tour and visit there often. I also have some dear friends and family there. But for me, it is a place where so much darkness remains, and the tentacles of oppression tried so hard to snare me before I escaped. As soon as I had the chance, I left. Arkansas beckoned, and I ran to her. She drew me unto her bosom, and I have rested and thrived there ever since. I have blossomed like a dogwood on the side of her mountains, and flown like an eagle over her valleys. I have loved her from the start. I will always love her. I have also spent a significant amount of time on the Great Plains and the Pine Ridge Indian reservation, where my Oglala Lakota tiyospaye (extended family) and friends reside. I love them deeply. They have given me so much. It is there that I am in my original homeland, and my feet disappear into the ground as my hair sways in the northern winds like the prairie grass. I am one with that land. It is in me, and I, in it. The oral history of my maternal Lakota ancestors speaks of abducted children sent away to Carlisle Indian School, and an eventual move to Michigan. My mixed-blood Lakota voice has risen from the ashes of ancestral abuse and stolen heritage like the *Firebird* to reclaim what was taken. Yes, I grew up far away from the land of my Lakota relatives. Still, we are inseparable, even from afar. But my *home* is in the ancient Ozark Mountains, near Eureka Springs, Arkansas. Which is why, when people ask me the question, "Where are you from?" it can be tricky to answer. But I can guarantee, you will never hear me say that I am from Michigan, even though I was born there. Such are the complicated idiosyncrasies that come with a life so deeply affected by child abuse. For, beneath the smiling façade, lies a deep reservoir of tears borne of great darkness and suffering. I am an enigma. I am the gentle warrior. I will bend, but I will not break. I am like the willow that can withstand the strongest storm. I survived, I healed and I rose from the ashes. I reclaimed myself. Those who knew me then, would not know me now. I am made anew. I have regained my voice.

A few years back, I was invited by Percy White Plume to participate in the Chief Big Foot Memorial Ride, a sacrificial, ceremonial journey which traced the route our Lakota ancestors took on their way to Wounded Knee, where they would ultimately be massacred by the 7th Calvary on December 29th, 1890. Being a Lakota person of mixed ancestry who had never lived on the rez, that invite was more than an honor, it was as if the door on the tipi of the Lakota community had swung open and welcomed me inside. At that time, I was struggling with whether to continue performing and recording with the Native American flute, as I had been suffering some personal attacks and was growing weary of it. When I saddled up on that first day, it was minus 20 degrees, and the wind was howling at 40 mph. Having almost never ridden a horse, I was in for a harrowing, painful experience which would test my strength and challenge me to finally face my lifelong struggle with fear. Each day, before and after we rode, an Elder and spiritual leader named 'Chubbs' Thunderhawk would offer words and prayers. One thing he said that left an impression on me was that *"without a Lakota name, it is as if you do not exist."* Those words rang in my ears as I endured 135 miles on the back of a horse in the frigid South Dakota winter. Midway through the 8-day journey, while all the riders ate and chatted in the gymnasium in the small reservation village of Kyle, Chubbs approached me and asked me to play the flute for everyone. I was incredibly humbled. He asked me every night after that. At the end of the final day, there was a meal at Billy Mills Hall in Pine Ridge village. I'd made it the entire 135 miles and never fell off my horse! I had gone the distance and triumphed over my fear. I found strength and courage I did not know I had. As fate would have it, I ended up sitting right next to Chubbs that night. Again, he asked me to go get my flute so I could play for him and the other riders. I returned with my instrument and sat back down, and he turned to me and asked me a question I had been waiting my whole life to hear: "Do you have a Lakota name?" The answer was no. To which he replied, "I'm gonna give you a Lakota name." I could hardly believe my ears. He took a few minutes to contemplate, and then turned to me and said, "I give you the name, *Siyotanka* (Big/Great Flute)!" After that, he put his hand on my shoulder and spoke again. As he gestured to my flute, he said "that is a flute, but it is not *the* flute. *You* are the flute. Don't forget that." He then stood and announced to all within earshot that I had received my Lakota name, that I was part of the community, and that I belonged. *I belonged.* For so long I had wandered those reservation roads like a ghost. I had been invisible to my own people. Chubbs Thunderhawk had welcomed me inside. I was home at last. He then asked me to play for everyone. I hadn't gone to eat yet, but that was okay. I didn't care about eating at that moment. I was fuller inside than I had ever been. I closed my eyes and played with all my heart and soul. When I finished, I was surprised to find that someone had brought me a full plate of food with all the fixings. And in that moment, Wakantanka spoke and said: "Trust Me, use the gift you have been given, and I will feed you." And so it was that the Native American flute had reached through the blinding fog of abuse, loss and heartbreak and found me. When I picked up that first flute all those years ago, I could play. It was effortless. I never needed a lesson. Somehow, that ancient instrument *knew* me, and I innately understood. It was a beautiful mystery I could not articulate until that night on the rez, but deep inside I had always known I was *destined* to connect with that ancient woodwind; to give it the breath of my life force and share its healing voice with the world. To pour my tears into its hollow resonance, that others who hurt may hear, and know that they are not alone. That enchanted voice sang, and healed my spirit too. At last, I had found my *claiming breath.*

Free
~ Breaking the Chains ~

Now comes the moment of truth. There is a final step to being completely healed from the damage of abuse. And it can sometimes be the most difficult. It is also the least understood. The first two are well known: surviving, and then healing the wounds. But most of us stop there and never go any further. We can function and get by without taking that last step, but I wanted to do more than just 'get by' in my life. I wanted *victory*. I wanted to rise above victimization, and reach my full potential as a human being. If you are a survivor of abuse, and you want to experience a total liberation, I invite you to go the final mile.

My father had died, and my siblings and I were at the church where the funeral had taken place waiting for the meal to be served, when a friend of my dad named Joe said he wanted to talk to us. We met him in the parking lot. As the four of us gathered in a semi-circle, Joe began. As soon as he began to speak, it was obvious he had been drinking. But that was nothing compared to what came out of his mouth. Joe told us that now that our dad was gone, we would have to be sure and *take care of Emily*. That she would be alone, and would need us. Ohhhh the irony! We all stood there in dumbfounded disbelief. I was stunned, and rendered speechless. There was nothing we could say in response. The explanation for why we would certainly <u>not</u> be taking care of Emily was just too enormous for that occasion. And though I realize Joe was completely ignorant about the horrors that woman had inflicted on me and my brother and sisters, if I could go back in time to that moment, I would slap him for saying that to us. I drove away that day and never even glanced over my shoulder. I was angry. Nobody had ever noticed. Even after everything I had done during and afterward to announce to the world that Emily was an abuser, it was like it had all fallen on deaf ears. Take care of her? You have got to be kidding me! I was through pretending. I was finished with putting on a happy face so as to not cause someone discomfort or make a scene. No longer would I continue the charade with my silence. I was sick of playing games with something so terribly real. And I was tired of everybody acting like nothing had ever happened. I was <u>done</u>. I would never be silent again. That moment with Joe was the last time I would ever be muted. I never went to another reunion with my dad's family, because I was not going to sit there with Emily present and behave as if everything was okay. Everything was definitely *not* okay. Many on my dad's side knew enough about the abuse we four kids suffered to stand up for us and actually *do something* about it. But they never did. Emily should have been <u>banished,</u> not *invited* to family reunions! My absence has cost me. Relatives I used to be close to, no longer communicate with me, like *I'm* the one who deserves to be excommunicated. Some have even ridiculed me. It's sad, but I am happy with my life. I wanted to be authentic. I needed to be true to myself. And if being included in their lives meant I had to tamp down the truth to prevent them any discomfort, well then, I had no choice but to walk away. And that's what I did. I spread my wings, and flew. I was finally free.

A few months after my father's death, I was in Michigan on tour, and decided to stop by his grave to pay my respects. Upon my arrival to his burial site, I saw his headstone for the first time, and couldn't believe my eyes. Inlaid into the stone, was a photo of my dad *with Emily*. That's right; a picture of *her* was on my dad's grave marker. I nearly laughed out loud at the sick, audacity of it. It was over. I would never be able to visit my father's final resting place again without having to look at Emily. I walked away in disbelief. Then, about a year after my dad's passing, Mumma died while I was on tour in England. My mother had lived in nursing homes since she was in her 40s. As her prescription drug abuse and physical ailments got worse and worse, she became like a child, and early onset dementia crept in. I had assumed the role of parent for years, moving her from place to place because she would break some rule at a home, and get kicked out. It all took me back to when I was a child and the landlords were evicting us. A few years before her death, my mom met a man twice her age who she took a liking to. His name was Jack. Not long after they met, Mumma moved out of the nursing home and into his house. It was a strange arrangement, as it turned out that Jack was still married, but didn't live with his wife. And the house, oh my, the walls were stained yellow by the nicotine from endless cigarette smoking. The place looked like it should have been condemned. But that was where my mom wanted to be, and so I visited her there often. When my mother ended up in the hospital with 13 morphine patches on her upper body, it was unclear who had put them on. But it had happened on Jack's watch. I didn't blame him, because I knew my mom was surely complicit, being that she had been addicted to prescription drugs for over 20 years. When we got the call that Mumma had been hospitalized, I was about to embark on my very first overseas tour. We contacted the promoter and asked them to change the flights so we could drive to the hospital in Michigan, 1,000 miles away and see my mother. They agreed to do that for us. I had seen her hospitalized and watched her cheat death time and time again throughout the years, so I spoke with the doctor and asked him what he thought her chances were. The doctor, of course said there were no guarantees, but that – based on his observations – he thought she would be okay. I did too. I may have been deluding myself, but like I said, I had a history with it. So, I spent the day with her, brushing her hair and caressing her face as she drifted in and out of consciousness. Her life had been so hard. I understood so much about her pain. I just wanted to comfort her. At one point, she began to stir, and I leaned over and looked deep into my mother's eyes as she looked up at me, and mouthed the words *I love you* to her. Due to a bad mix of drugs given to her during one of her past hospital visits, Mumma had been deaf for years, but she could read my lips like a pro. She saw my words, nodded her head and blinked her eyes, and I knew she understood. Walking out of that hospital that night was one of the hardest things I have ever done. But I *really did believe*, in my heart of hearts, that my mom was going to bounce back like she had always done before. I awoke a few days later in England to an email from my brother – Mumma was gone. I never felt so alone, so disconnected. I went outside and looked up at the gray sky, reaching for my sadness, but I couldn't find it. I was numb. I was empty. I would miss my own mother's funeral. A few days later I gave a concert in West Sussex. Nobody knew I had just lost my mother. Afterward, there was a lady at the end of the 'meet and greet' line who wanted to share something with me. Assuring me that she wasn't crazy, she told me she had seen something supernatural during my show; that, during one of my songs, a cloud had appeared over my head, and there was a young woman in that cloud with long dark hair, who was dancing and kept saying the same thing over and over: *don't be sad, I can dance again, and I can hear the music.* That lady was the only one that night, who ever heard that my mother had just died, because after she shared her vision with me, I told her. I had left for Europe with an '*I love you*' into my mother's eyes. I returned to a fresh grave with no marker. My siblings and I were still planning to get a headstone designed. Our idea was to have "Mumma" inscribed on it. A short time later I was back in Michigan, and swung by the cemetery to stop at my mom's burial site. As I walked up to it, I was flabbergasted to find that there was a gravestone there. It read "*My Sweetheart*"!? I was incredulous. Without asking any of her children for permission, Jack – who had only known her for maybe a year – had put a headstone on my mother's final resting place. I could not believe it. First, my father's grave, and now my mother's? It was like some kind of a sick joke. So much had been denied us. Could we not even have this one thing? Was it too much to ask? That headstone was the final insult. I could take it no more. I walked away from Mumma's grave that day, and I have never been back. Neither have I ever returned to my dad's. My siblings and I have never replaced our mother's headstone. Not because we don't want to, but I suppose for the same reasons I don't visit my parents' gravesites; there is a lot of hurt in those places and we've had our fill of that. We just want to be free from it. And so, I let my parents go. I released them from my perceptions, and from my judgments. I set them free, and in doing so, liberated my spirit. I don't need to visit their graves, because they are not there anyway. They have taken flight, and slipped beyond the veil to the spirit world, which touches my soul now and again, and allows me to see them in the light.

Writing this book has forced me to think about the awful people who abused me as a child more than I have in years – especially Emily. Normally, these days, she never crosses my mind. I almost never think about her. You see, I released her too. That's right; I made the decision not to occupy space in my psyche with images and memories of her. I realized long ago that if I were ever to be completely healed and fully free, I would have to let it all go. I did not forgive her. I *pardoned* her. Although she is guilty, and committed despicable crimes, I will not imprison her in my mind. And so, she has become nothing. Because, though my dad and Mumma have passed away, it is *she* who is dead, as she lives no longer in the sphere of my world. My friends, no matter who or what has hurt you in this life, if you are ever to find your way to liberation from the torment of that pain, you must let the tormentor go. You must release them. Not because they are innocent, but because *you* are. So, reach inside to where you have them locked up, turn the key, and walk away.

And so it was that I found myself in the broken down craggy place that day, with a cardinal singing to me. Of all the beautiful spots in that sacred area, Wakantanka had led me here, where I would finally complete my journey of healing, and be shown my hidden medicine. Before I went home that night, I had a brief moment with a black snake. I asked one of the medicine people about it, and was told to offer tobacco and pray, because "transformation was coming". I did so, and then headed out. I woke up the next day with over 300 chigger bites all over my body from the waist down. It was horrible. The itching would not relent, and I barely got any sleep for 3 nights in a row. On the 4th night, I thought I was going to lose my mind, when suddenly I saw a strange light and caught a familiar scent in my bedroom. I couldn't explain it, but I could actually *smell* my mother. I felt her essence touch mine, and detected a soft whisper in my soul. A question formed, and was imparted; "What would you do to make your suffering stop?" I answered, *"Anything"*. The gentle reply washed over me in waves; "Now you understand." I don't recall how, but I drifted off to sleep after that, and awoke the next morning to find that the itching had stopped. I had come full circle, and a great wisdom had been shown to me. Hidden in the scars of abuse was a medicine so powerful that it could heal the world. I did not inflict those wounds. Somebody awful had done those things. But the surviving, the healing and the releasing – that was all me. *I did that*. And now, at long last, I understood. I would have to accept my scars if I was to ever be free. I needed to embrace them, honor them and own them. They were *mine*. Deep within them all was my story, my humanity, and my purpose. During the making of my *Hidden Medicine* album, I underwent what was supposed to be a simple, in-office surgery. 20 years earlier, I had gotten sun poisoning on my chest during a trip to Florida. Decades later that damage had resulted in a small basal cell carcinoma scab on my left pectoral just above my nipple, right over my heart. As I had done with my urinary tract infection all those years ago, I procrastinated and avoided facing it. Old habits die hard. After a few years of prompting from my doctor during annual checkups, I finally heeded her advice and made an appointment with a skin cancer physician who I will call 'Doctor H' to have it removed. What was supposed to be a reasonably small procedure with minimal healing time devolved into a months-long nightmare that nearly cost me my life. Seven days after I had gone home with a terribly long stitched-up wound, it began bleeding and wouldn't stop. Something had gone wrong. My Apache friend and brother from Kansas City, Dr. Jesse, had seen the stitches, and had some concerns about what he saw. I ended up back at Doctor H's office to have the surgery completely redone. During the second procedure, I felt a burning sensation, and mentioned it, but the doctor just placated me. Afterward, I asked how long I could leave the bandage on, and was told it could stay on as long as I wanted, even until the stitches came out, which was at least 10 days. I didn't know it then, but that was terrible medical advice. I went home, and by the next day I was in blinding agony. Peggy called the doctor's office to ask why, because I hadn't hurt like that the first time. They told her that it was probably because I'd had two surgeries on the same area, and then gave me a prescription for pain pills. Three days later, I was in Kansas City to drop my grandson off at the airport. He had been with us for a visit, and I had been miserable the entire time. We had planned to meet Dr. Jesse for lunch on the way back. As sure as I sit here now, I can tell you that, had I not met my friend for lunch that day, I would be dead. During the meal, he invited me to see his office, and offered to change my bandage. I was reluctant, as I had intended to leave it on longer, based on what I had been told after that second surgery. But he and Peggy insisted, so I agreed. We finished eating, and drove to his office. After he gave me a little tour, I sat down so he could change the dressing on my wound. But when he peeled back the tape, he immediately told me I was in trouble. It looked like soup under that gauze. My wound was oozing with what would turn out to be a staph infection (which explained the burning sensation I felt during the 2nd surgery), and my body suddenly began to feel cold and nauseated. Dr. Jesse was very worried that I might have developed sepsis, and that I was going into septic shock right there in his office, and could die as a result. He took immediate action, and put me through 25 minutes of horrendous torture as he manually pushed and squeezed the infection out of my wound. The pain was horrific, but he never relented. He knew my very life was on the line. After a few more cleansing procedures and an internal gauze packing, he sent me home freshly bandaged up, and arranged for a powerful antibiotic. Over the next several months that wound would go through a terribly hideous healing process. But in the end, it healed, and I am left with a nasty scar over my heart. On the way home from Kansas City that night, Dr. Jesse sent me a text that said simply, *sweet, hidden medicine*. After the wound finally closed, my wife told me she loved my new scar! And guess what, so do I. That scar is the physical manifestation of all I have survived in my life. Dr. Jesse saved me that night. But I had also saved myself. I was free. Joy and happiness returned. I found the way back to my quiet place in the sacred woods, and the birds were singing their songs of hope to me again. The scared, sensitive boy of long ago had become a courageous, sensitive man. I had survived. I had healed. And I was victorious. I had danced with the shadows and lost my innocence.... endured the suffering and cried in the rain.... ran from the terror and searched for love.... found my voice and faced my affliction.... rose from the ashes and took back my life.... and released my pain to set myself free. Yes, those scars were indeed my power. And I would draw a healing salve from their jagged truth as I poured out the enchanted song of my sacred vision – to reach out to a hurting world, with *Hidden Medicine*.